Editor-in-Chief and Founder:
 Lyndon H. LaRouche, Jr.
Editorial Board: *Lyndon H. LaRouche, Jr. , Helga
 Zepp-LaRouche, Robert Ingraham, Tony
 Papert, Gerald Rose, Dennis Small, Jeffrey
 Steinberg, William Wertz*
Co-Editors: *Robert Ingraham, Tony Papert*
Managing Editor: *Nancy Spannaus*
Technology: *Marsha Freeman*
Books: *Katherine Notley*
Ebooks: *Richard Burden*
Graphics: *Alan Yue*
Photos: *Stuart Lewis*
Circulation Manager: *Stanley Ezrol*

INTELLIGENCE DIRECTORS
Counterintelligence: *Jeffrey Steinberg, Michele
 Steinberg*
Economics: *John Hoefle, Marcia Merry Baker,
 Paul Gallagher*
History: *Anton Chaitkin*
Ibero-America: *Dennis Small*
Russia and Eastern Europe: *Rachel Douglas*
United States: *Debra Freeman*

INTERNATIONAL BUREAUS
Bogotá: *Miriam Redondo*
Berlin: *Rainer Apel*
Copenhagen: *Tom Gillesberg*
Houston: *Harley Schlanger*
Lima: *Sara Madueño*
Melbourne: *Robert Barwick*
Mexico City: *Gerardo Castilleja Chávez*
New Delhi: *Ramtanu Maitra*
Paris: *Christine Bierre*
Stockholm: *Ulf Sandmark*
United Nations, N.Y.C.: *Leni Rubinstein*
Washington, D.C.: *William Jones*
Wiesbaden: *Göran Haglund*

ON THE WEB
e-mail: eirns@larouchepub.com
www.larouchepub.com
www.executiveintelligencereview.com
www.larouchepub.com/eiw
Webmaster: *John Sigerson*
Assistant Webmaster: *George Hollis*
Editor, Arabic-language edition: *Hussein Askary*

EIR (ISSN 0273-6314) *is published weekly
(50 issues), by EIR News Service, Inc.,
P.O. Box 17390, Washington, D.C. 20041-0390.
(703) 297-8434*

European Headquarters: E.I.R. GmbH, Postfach
Bahnstrasse 9a, D-65205, Wiesbaden, Germany
Tel: 49-611-73650
Homepage: http://www.eir.de
e-mail: info@eir.de
Director: Georg Neudecker

Montreal, Canada: 514-461-1557
eir@eircanada.ca

Denmark: EIR - Danmark, Sankt Knuds Vej 11,
basement left, DK-1903 Frederiksberg, Denmark.
Tel.: +45 35 43 60 40, Fax: +45 35 43 87 57. e-mail:
eirdk@hotmail.com.

Mexico City: EIR, Sor Juana Inés de la Cruz 242-2
Col. Agricultura C.P. 11360
Delegación M. Hidalgo, México D.F.
Tel. (5525) 5318-2301
eirmexico@gmail.com

Canada Post Publication Sales Agreement
#40683579

Postmaster: Send all address changes to *EIR*, P.O.
Box 17390, Washington, D.C. 20041-0390.

Signed articles in *EIR* represent the views of the authors,
and not necessarily those of the Editorial Board.

London Drives for War

EDITORIAL

British Stand Exposed as Source of The War Drive: Their Meddling Must End!

by Harley Schlanger

April 14—In the face of an ongoing deluge of lies and disinformation about Russia, coming from the institutions of the British Empire and its pathetic mouthpieces, there are two points of emphasis which must not be forgotten: first, that the City of London and Wall Street, the centers of power of the Empire, are hopelessly bankrupt, and are willing to risk thermonuclear war to maintain their global dominance; and second, that the great fear of those running the collapsing empire comes from the emergence of a New Paradigm, which rejects their geopolitical manipulations, and is based instead on cooperation between the United States, on the one side, and Russia and China on the other. The potential for realizing this New Paradigm has increased since the election of President Trump, with his promise to reverse the policy of regime change wars launched by his predecessors, Bush and Obama.

It is this potential which has been the target of the British-directed campaign against Trump, in first accusing him of being a *de facto* agent under the control of Putin, and then delivering fake intelligence to him, which convinced him to order a cruise missile strike against the Shayrat air base in Syria.

These two points were

U.S. Secretary of State Rex Tillerson and Russian President Vladimir Putin.

en.kremlin.ru

highlighted in an exchange between British UN Ambassador Matthew Rycroft, and Russia's Acting Ambassador Vladimir Safronkov, during the United Nations Security Council debate on April 12, on yet another British sponsored resolution condemning the Assad government in Syria. Rycroft launched a vitriolic diatribe against Russia, blaming Russia for the deaths of Syrian civilians from chemical weapons, due to its continued support for Assad.

Safronkov responded sharply: "What you are afraid of is that we [Russia] might work with the United States. That's what you lose sleep over." He continued, saying the United Kingdom is more focused on regime change than in aiding the Syrian people, and instead "invite illegal armed groups to London." The latter point is a clear reference to British support for groups such as the "White Helmets," a phony aid group infiltrated by jihadists terrorists, which was the main source for the allegations that it was Assad's forces which used chemical weapons which killed civilians in Khan Shaykhun.

In his denunciation of the Queen's representative at the UN, Safronkov correctly identified the British as the instigator of the crisis that put the world on the edge of nuclear war. In doing so, he echoed U.S. statesman Lyndon LaRouche who warned U.S. President Trump that he must break out of the trap set by the British, by meeting immediately with Russian President Putin to reverse the march toward war. LaRouche reminded Trump that the British have been the enemy of this nation since its beginnings, and have repeatedly engaged in efforts to sabotage the American System of economics, which Trump has been championing.

"The British Empire has been the enemy of mankind for a long time," LaRouche said, "Shut down the British System! The U.S. is a *nation*—always has been a nation... so we must not submit." He added that Trump must clean out the nest of British advocates of confrontation with Russia who are responsible for pushing the false reports of Assad's responsibility for using chemical weapons. But, above all, he must meet with Putin as soon as possible.

Tillerson-Putin Meeting

A major step in this direction occurred on April 12, when U.S. Secretary of State Rex Tillerson met in Moscow with Russian Foreign Minister Sergey Lavrov, and then with President Putin. An attempt to sabotage that meeting had been undertaken by Britain's Foreign Secretary Boris Johnson, who demanded that the G7 foreign ministers, meeting in Italy, demand new sanctions against Russia, claiming Russian complicity in the alleged Syrian chemical weapons attack. Johnson intended that Tillerson use the scheduled meeting in Moscow to deliver an ultimatum to the Russians, that they would face new, tougher sanctions, unless they dropped support for Assad.

This ploy was thwarted by a rare show of good sense, as several European governments, including Germany and Italy, joined with Japan in rejecting Johnson's demand. Instead, they demanded a full UN investigation to determine the facts about the chemical weapons incident.

Reports from the Tillerson-Lavrov meeting, and the later meeting with Putin, indicate that, despite some tough language from both sides, progress was made in the discussions. While acknowledging that differences between the two nations exist, a "working group" will be established, to address those differences, and that the memorandum on de-confliction, to avoid possible inadvertent attacks on each others' forces in the region— which had been suspended by Russia after the U.S. mis-

sile attack—would likely be restored.

In his comments, Lavrov spoke of the "shared responsibility" of the two nations, and added, "We understand each other better after today's talks." He said the U.S. and Russia "are not worlds apart" on many key issues, but reviewed Russian concerns over recent U.S. and NATO interventions, including in Yugoslavia and Libya. He reiterated Russia's contention that the U.S. has presented "no proof" of Assad's responsibility for the chemical attack, and reminded Tillerson that there must be a "presumption of innocence" until a full investigation has been conducted.

While Tillerson stuck to the story that there is "conclusive" evidence of Assad's guilt, he stated that the "low level of trust between our two countries" is a problem, and that the "world's two foremost nuclear powers cannot have this kind of relationship... We need to attempt to put an end to this steady degradation." He added that the two-hour meeting with Putin was "productive."

It is worth noting that, prior to the British efforts to blame Assad for the chemical weapon attack, Tillerson had stated that the U.S. no longer was committed to regime change in Syria, which had been a key part of Trump's pledge, during the campaign— to put an end to the regime change wars of Bush and Obama.

For his part, Trump seems to have stepped back from the confrontation the British intended to provoke, despite continuing efforts by the neocons to escalate, including reviving the plan to move 150,000 U.S. troops into Syria. Asked about the possibility of escalating against Assad, the President told *Fox Business News*, "Are we going to get involved in Syria? No." And following the Tillerson meetings in Moscow, he tweeted, "Things will work out fine between the USA and Russia."

Must Take on the Brits

Despite such sentiments, there can be no secure peace without going after the British instigators of the anti-Trump, anti-Russian operations, as they will not stop until Trump is either completely submissive to their intentions, or ousted. This news service has documented the role of British intelligence in directing the anti-Trump campaign. Among the more obvious lies is its authorship of the charge that the Russians control Trump through sexual blackmail—the notorious dossier produced by "former" MI6 operative Christopher Steele, in collaboration with Trump's enemies in the

Republican Party, the Clinton campaign, and the FBI. Despite the near-universal recognition of that dossier being a complete fraud, there are still efforts by the media, and by Congressmen from both parties, to bring Steele before Congressional committees to testify.

Additional new evidence has been forthcoming of the overall role of the British in targeting Trump. On April 13, the *Guardian* confirms that the GCHQ, the coordinating center of British intelligence, began investigating "suspicious 'interactions' between figures connected to Trump and known or suspected Russian agents," that they picked up from surveillance in the summer of 2015, then passed on to U.S. intelligence agencies. In the summer of 2016, the head of GCHQ, Robert Hannigan, delivered material directly to CIA Director and Obama intimate John Brennan, who used it "to launch a major inter-agency investigation." That investigation, or rather witch-hunt, is continuing, with the aim of destroying the Trump presidency.

Another example is an April 13 article in the *Daily Mail*, which says that former MI6 chief Sir Richard Dearlove "suggests," without offering any evidence, that Trump received money from Russians in 2008. Sir Richard was head of MI6 in 2002, when his agency produced the dossier which asserted that Saddam Hussein had weapons of mass destruction. He personally wrote the forward to the dossier, in which he stated that the threat from Saddam "was beyond doubt." He then delivered the dossier to Tony Blair, who joined with George W. Bush in using this lying dossier to justify the invasion of Iraq, which triggered the broader regional war and terrorist recruitment which threatens the world today.

In addition to Russian Acting UN Ambassador Safronkov's direct identification of the British role in concocting the Syrian provocation, the former British Ambassador to Syria, Peter Ford, stunned a BBC interviewer by saying he did not believe the so-called intelligence that led to Trump's attack. The *Daily Mail* reported on this interview on April 11, under the headline, "Truth Bomb Dropped Live on BBC by British Ambassador Goes Viral." When challenged by the BBC interviewer, who asked of the charges against Assad, "That's a statement of fact, right?," Ford calmly replied, "It's a myth.... It's a statement of non-fact."

He said that, in the run-up to the Iraq war, "The experts... were convinced that Saddam had weapons of mass destruction.... They were all wrong. It's possible that they are wrong in this instance as well. That they are just looking for a pretext to attack Syria." He called the chemical weapons attack a "fake flag" that may have been done by the terrorists, to lead to an escalation against Assad, and warned that the terrorists may launch another chemical weapons attack, to provoke further retaliation.

There is a growing number of individuals and institutions coming forward to challenge the Assad-did-it line. Among the most significant is weapons expert Ted Postol, who issued a 14-page report to thoroughly refute the four-page dossier released by the White House that claims to prove Assad's responsibility. Postol concludes that the White House report "does not provide any evidence whatsoever that the U.S. government has concrete knowledge" of the government of Syria's responsibility for the attack.

Another significant statement against the lurch toward war comes from the Veteran Intelligence Professionals for Sanity (VIPS), in an open letter to President Trump. Signed by twenty-four retired intelligence and military officers and released under the heading, "Trump Should Rethink Syria Escalation," they say they are writing "to give you an unambiguous warning of the threat of armed hostilities with Russia—with the risk of escalation to nuclear war." Also joining those warning of the danger is retired Col. Lawrence Wilkerson, former chief of staff of U.S. Secretary of State Colin Powell, who has repeatedly referred to Powell's use of the Blair dossier in his address to the UN as a fraud. Wilkerson demands that Tillerson apologize to Lavrov for his charges against Russia.

While the interventions of Postol, Wilkerson and the VIPS are significant, as they establish a standard of truth as essential before missiles are launched, they do not identify the key role of the British. In his comments, LaRouche has insisted that such an omission can be fatal.

What we are witnessing, LaRouche said, in the escalation against Syria and Russia, is "treason against the U.S. from the inside, using forces inside the government to destroy that government. No British institution has the right to meddle in American affairs. Obama is an example of this evil. Mankind has to learn to fight, to shut down things that are wrong. The British Empire is wrong.... People must have the guts to do what must be done. The time has come to crush this thing. Get this nation and other nations to agree to that."

EIR Contents

www.larouchepub.com Volume 44, Number 16, April 21, 2017

Cover This Week

U.S. Air Force B-52 Stratofortress leads a formation of NATO aircraft over the Baltic Sea, June 9, 2016.

U.S. Air Force photo/Senior airman Erin Babis

I. China, the United States, and the World

SCHILLER INSTITUTE CONFERENCE, NEW YORK

U.S.-China Cooperation on The Belt and Road Initiative

The Schiller Institute held a conference in New York City on April 13-14, 2017, entitled: "U.S.-China Cooperation on the Belt and Road Initiative and Corresponding Ideas in Chinese and Western Philosophy." The following are transcripts of the first four presentations in Panel I on April 13, namely:

- Justin Yu, head, Chinese Chamber of Commerce of New York City,
- Virginia Senator Richard Black,
- Helga Zepp-LaRouche,
- Mme. Zhang Meifang, the Deputy Consul General, at the Consulate General of the People's Republic of China in New York.

EIRNS/Jason Ross

Dr. Patrick Ho addressing the conference.

Dennis Speed: My name is Dennis Speed, and on behalf of the Schiller Institute and the Foundation for the Revival of Classical Culture, I'd like to welcome you to today's conference: "U.S.-China Cooperation on the Belt and Road Initiative and Corresponding Ideas in Chinese and Western Philosophy."

Justin Yu

I'm going first start us off by reading a statement of greetings from the Chinese Chamber of Commerce of New York City. It says:

"The Chinese Chamber of Commerce of New York City offers its welcome and thanks for the two-day conference of the Schiller Institute to present to an Ameri-

can audience the proposal for the United States to join China in helping to lead in the project to develop the Belt and Road across the Eurasian continent. We are honored and delighted that the founder of the Schiller Institute, Helga Zepp-LaRouche, will address the conference both days, as she is widely recognized as one of the creators and leading proponents of the project. That she will be joined by prominent representatives of China and other nations and international organizations, makes this occasion unique.

"The success of this conference could have the beneficial effect of leading the United States to join in this great project for the benefit of the globe. Sadly, too many still think in terms of geopolitical competition,

Some of the conference attendees between sessions.

EIRNS/Jason Ross

rather than mutual benefit, or what Chinese President Xi Jinping calls 'win-win' collaboration. At this time in history, conflict among leading nations is to be avoided, as its consequences are horrific for the future of mankind.

"We offer our welcome, and wish you great success."

—Justin Yu, head, Chinese Chamber of Commerce of New York City

Speed: We're going to play a welcome and a greeting for the conference from State Senator Richard Black of Virginia; and you'll see it here on the monitor.

Virginia Senator Richard Black

Sen. Richard Black: I'm Senator Richard H. Black. I'm very pleased to once again introduce you to the Schiller Institute's presentation on the Silk Road,— the New Paradigm for a world order.

A little bit of my background: I was in Syria last April, right after the Syrian military had liberated Palmyra. I went to Palmyra, and then with a heavily armored convoy, we went out into ISIS-controlled territory. So, I've seen the ground, and also I have met a vast number of the officials. I met with President Bashar al-Assad; I told him that I regretted that his wife would not be there, and ten minutes later, his wife Asma al-Assad walked in—truly a most gracious and delightful woman. We earlier had met with General [Michel] Aoun, who has since been named the President of Lebanon. So, we had a very productive time over there, and learned a great deal. But my background with Syria was not simply a trip over there; it was six years of study, and very intensely following the events occurring in Syria. I'm very aware of the way that the war began, and the terrible tragedy it has created. The Western

countries and many of the Gulf State countries have made fabulous profits from the manipulation of the oil industry and also from war profiteering. It really is my desire to see this end, and I think this is what Helga La-Rouche is going to discuss during this conference.

I am so distressed by our recent missile attacks on Syria. I have defied anyone to give me a motive for Syria to have used a poison gas attack. I think, to some extent, the White House has felt a bit defensive about this because they have found it necessary to go on the media and to refute my challenges. At the same time that we have this very brutal war—it was not a natural uprising in Syria: It was a coming together in a deliberate attempt by covert agencies to topple the government of Syria. We had toppled the government of Libya. Now we see a very brutal war in Yemen, in which the Saudi Arabians are attempting to force a puppet government on the legitimate government in the capital city of Sana'a. All of this is so unnecessary; there's such vast slaughter and bloodshed, such tremendous destruction of property—factories, homes, and priceless artifacts that can never possibly be replaced. This time of destruction, bloodshed, hatred among peoples needs to come to an end.

I think that what the Schiller Institute is offering is an opportunity, through the Silk Road and the New Paradigm for the world, to offer a new way for the global oligarchs to profit. But at the same time, the Silk Road not only will enrich the handful of elites who propagate the wars and the destruction around the world; but it will also be able to enrich the common man. This is what we want; this brings stability, it brings happiness to the millions rather than just immense wealth to just the few. So, we welcome you to the Schiller Institute's presentation. I'm Senator Richard Black, and very pleased to have you here. Thank you for your attendance.

HELGA ZEPP-LAROUCHE

Whither the U.S.: Nuclear War Or New Silk Road?

Dennis Speed: In June 1996, our keynote speaker appeared in Beijing at a conference which discussed the concept of the New Silk Road. She, and her husband Lyndon LaRouche, had designed—a bit earlier than that conference, starting in 1989—a concept of development and peace that would unify East and West. It had other names earlier—the European Triangle was one such name, and then later it was extended to Asia as the Eurasian Land-Bridge. A fight to make that concept real was begun at that time. During the period between June 1996 and January/February 1997, she was

EIRNS/Jason Ross
Helga Zepp-LaRouche

given the name the "Silk Road Lady." At the end of 2014, a new report and a new evaluation was supplied by the Schiller Institute and published by *Executive Intelligence Review*; it was called "The New Silk Road Becomes the World Land-Bridge." In this time of great turmoil, the capacity to concentrate and to focus on what the true goals of mankind and mankind's future are, is of utmost importance. It is specifically important for Americans to hear that perspective from the eyes of people who consider themselves to be Americans in character and in principle. That's the way that the Schiller Institute, from the time of its inception, has thought; it has always been from that time until now my great honor to introduce on whatever occasion it requires, the founder and leader of the Schiller Institute, Helga Zepp-LaRouche.

Helga Zepp-LaRouche: Dear friends of the Schiller Institute, when we designed the title of this conference—and I hope I am not mistaken, because you gave a different name—I had the title of "Whither the United States? Nuclear War or New Silk Road?" We did not have exactly an inkling at that time that the seed of both options would be condensed in the two-day summit between President Trump and President Xi Jinping in Florida just a little while ago. But the first day of this summit was very positive. It was reported that the chemistry between the two Presidents was very good; President Trump called it an outstanding relationship and "lots of possibilities to get rid of potentially bad problems," hoping that they will go away. President Xi Jinping, for his part, said that he received a very warm reception; that they had an in-depth communication, and he stressed the unique importance of the U.S.-Sino relationship. And, which is very important, he offered to the United States to join the Belt and Road Initiative, the New Silk Road. As many of you may know, I had called earlier that we must have a nationwide mobilization in the entire United States, that the United States must join in this fantastic new project.

Obviously, what happened is not yet totally clear. Trump did not say anything explicitly; he didn't take up the offer. But if he does, and I said this a little while ago—people were actually quite shocked to hear me say that, and I still say that despite what happened in the recent days: If he [President Xi] can convince President Trump to take up the offer to join with China and the other nations in the New Silk Road, he can become one of the greatest Presidents in the history of the United States.

In light of what happened with the air strikes against Syria, many people may wonder why I'm still saying this, but I'm absolutely convinced of it. Because if we can get the United States to join and cooperate—and later I will elaborate what that will mean—it would mean to overcome geopolitics, which has been the source of two world wars in the past century. The United States would join what President Xi Jinping all the time calls a community for the shared future of mankind, and it would indeed begin a new era of mankind and eliminate the danger of nuclear war.

The first day went very positively, but then during the night to Friday, the United States launched the military strike into Syria under the pretext that the Syrian government had allegedly used chemical weapons in the province of Idlib, which caused the deaths of civilians, babies. But no proof was presented. It was immediately contradicted by many ex-intelligence experts, saying this was a typical false-flag operation. Fortunately, President Xi Jinping maintained his countenance; he did not leave. They stayed for the second day and concluded agreements to have a new Cabinet-level framework for negotiations and continue a dialogue on four pillars: First, a diplomatic and security dialogue; then, a comprehensive economic dialogue; a law-enforcement and cyber-security dialogue; and a dialogue concerning social and cultural issues.

Now this was obviously not our demand, but it opens the door. As we have seen in recent phone calls between the two Presidents, especially as a consequence of these strikes against Syria, the North Korean crisis is flaring up in a very dangerous way. At least the two Presidents got on the phone, and at times like this, this is extremely important.

What happened is a de facto coup d'état inside the United States, which has two elements. One is the false-flag operation in Syria, combined with what one could call a palace coup inside the administration. This coup—and I will elaborate on that also—is a British intelligence operation; and it must be recognized as such in order to liberate President Trump from this great danger. If you look at the chronology of what happened, March 30, both Secretary of State [Rex] Tillerson and UN Ambassador Nikki Haley said very clearly that it is no longer an option of the United States to oust President Assad, our priority is to fight terrorism and ISIS. One day later, the American Secretary of Defense [James] Mattis was in London and gave a press conference with the British Defence Minister, Michael Fallon, where he praised the British global role worldwide and threatened Russia, saying they are responsible for manipulations of the elections in the United States and

Europe. On the same day, British Foreign Minister Boris Johnson, who already in December had called for a joint U.S. military attack on Syria, had to admit that the U.K. investigation about Russian interference in the U.S. election had produced no result.

The Chemical Attack

Then on April 4, there were the first reports about the bombing attacks on Idlib province with chemical weapons. The next morning, President Trump received his daily intelligence brief, and this brief said it was an attack with chemical weapons by the Syrian government. And as evidence, they showed photographs and videos of people dying, apparently from chemical poisoning. The source of this was an organization called the White Helmets. The following two days, there were National Security Council meetings in Washington, and on the same day, the House Intelligence Committee chair, Representative [Devin] Nunes [R-CA], recused himself from the investigation into the two narratives: one narrative being that Russia had helped Trump to become President; the other narrative being that the Deep State in the United States has been leaking classified information about Americans being spied on. These two narratives are in a showdown, and Nunes was on the right track, because he had received in meetings in the Old Executive Building, proof that there was such cooperation with British intelligence on this matter. So, he was accused by Citizens for Responsibility and Ethics in Washington, MoveOn.org Civic Action, and other groups, in a complaint to the House Office of Congressional Ethics, that he had not briefed [House Intelligence Committee ranking member] Adam Schiff [D-CA] first, but the President. In any case, he thought he had to recuse himself. It turns out that this Committee for Responsibility and Ethics in Washington is financed entirely by the British; George Soros, among others. Then the next day, on April 5, [White House Chief Strategist Steve] Bannon, the campaign advisor of Trump, was removed from the National Security Council. It is generally known that he opposed the attack against Syria. On April 6, in the middle of the summit with President Xi, when the decision was taken to attack the Syrian airbase with 60 Tomahawk missiles, Michael Fallon, the British Defence Minister, bragged that he was in constant communication with the United States on all levels—before the strike, after the strike—discussing the options. So, this immediately brought the world to the verge of a serious showdown with Russia. Many security experts, includ-

Direction of lethal plume on April 4, 2017 between 3 and 6 a.m., assuming the munition crater identified by the White House is actually the sarin dispersal site.

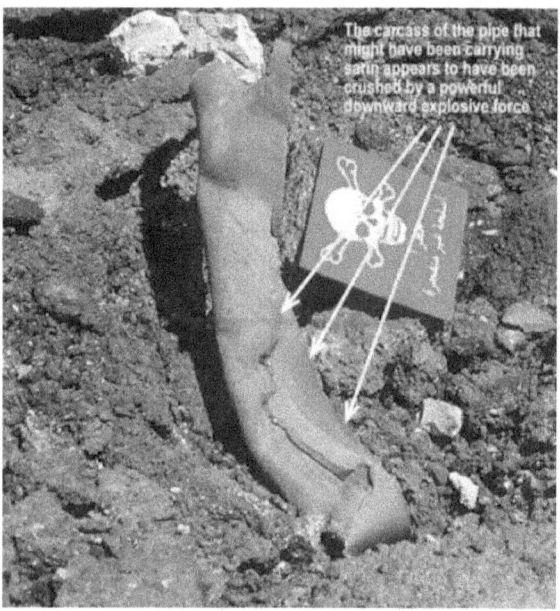

Deformation of sarin containing pipe and crater from the action of the explosive charge placed on top of the pipe.

ing Scott Ritter, who is a senior chemical weapons inspector who had numerous times in the past denounced the White Helmets, pointing out that the White Helmets were associated with al-Qaeda, refuted this immediately.

This organization, the White Helmets, was founded by a retired British military officer, James Le Mesurier; it receives $30 million from the British Defence Ministry, but also from the U.S. State Department. They have quite a portfolio of $100 million, and they have been seen in videos assisting al-Qaeda in the execution of Syrian soldiers. The idea that this evidence, that it was the Syrian government who did that, was refuted two days ago by a very prominent nuclear weapons expert, MIT Professor Ted Postol, who was the single person who, in 2013, proved that the apparent use of chemical weapons at that time was not done by the Syrian government, but by rebel groups. He responded to the four-page memorandum by the White House, claiming that they had absolutely undebatable proof that it was the Syrian government. He published a 14-page paper in which he used Google Earth material and photographs that are generally made available, to say that by analyzing the pipe out of which the so-called chemical gas came, it could not have been dropped by an airplane, but it had been delivered by other ways. Here he shows some more technical details. This is now a situation where yesterday Russian Foreign Minister [Sergey] Lavrov and President [Vladimir] Putin met with Secretary of State Tillerson; they had five hours of discussion, and with President Putin two more hours of dis-

cussion. The White House maintained the story that they have the proof that this was the Syrian government; the Russian government said no, we need an international investigation immediately, because you cannot condemn somebody where the evidence is so absolutely ludicrous.

The site where the [chemical] attack occurred was held by an organization called Liwa al-Aqsa; and the Syrian government and also the Russian government maintain that the object which was hit was a storage place for chemical weapons that are produced by the rebels. The logic of the whole thing is also clear. Remember that in 2013, there was a tremendous intervention with Russian help; the Syrian government agreed to dismantle its entire chemical weapons stockpile. It was destroyed. Eight of ten production places were destroyed, and two remained in the area where the rebels are. The Syrian ambassador to the United Nations put out a statement yesterday saying that he sent 80 letters to the UN Security Council, giving them data on where the rebels were using this; where it came from—even Turkish intelligence helped. So why would President Assad, who is currently, with the help of Russia, winning the battle on all fronts, why would he risk this very favorable situation by using chemical weapons against a target which is of *no* military use whatsoever? Why would Russia, which has put a lot of political investment in getting the Syrian government to dismantle its chemical weapons, why would they idly sit by and

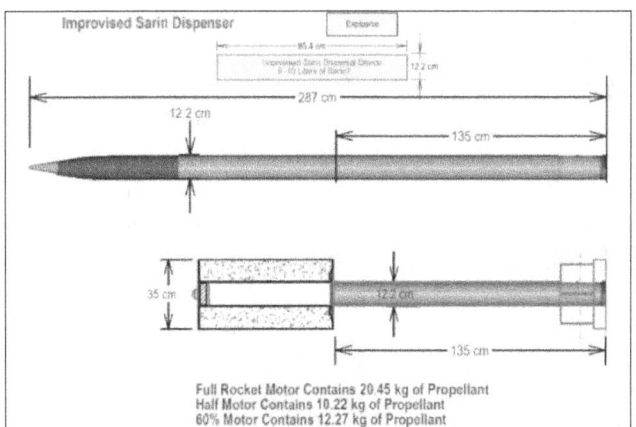

The ground-placed improvised sarin dispersal device is shown next to a standard 122 mm artillery rocket. The explosive placed on top of the pipe would cause it to be suddenly crushed, like a tube of toothpaste hit by a mallet. The sarin would be sprayed out from the metal tube.

allow this to happen? It just does not make any sense at all.

What's Going On?

There is no evidence. If there were any evidence, the U.S. would have presented it already; but the latest statement from the United States is that they have to protect their "methods and sources." To take pictures like that from the air, from satellites, is not such a secret thing. This is now a serious problem, because there are many experts, including top Mideast experts in Europe, who say that this military strike [on the Syrian airbase] was completely illegal; it had no UN mandate, it had no Congressional legitimization, it had not the article of legitimate self-defense according to Article 51 of the UN Charter. If there are further attacks—and President Putin has warned already that the U.S. attack encourages other rebel groups to do other such operations in order to lure the United States more into this conflict—this could then bring a showdown with Russia in the short term.

It also has relevance for NATO. There was a judge of a federal court in Germany who made the point that if it were to come to a military confrontation between the United States and Russia over this issue, NATO members could not be asked to come to the defense of the United States according to Article 5 of the NATO Charter; because if a force reacts to an aggression, this article does not apply.

So, it's a very hot situation. But one of the most incredible things is that the same international corps of neo-cons and neo-liberals who immediately after the election victory of Trump, used the most inciting words for Trump—calling him a fascist, a hate preacher, an unstable sociopath, an incompetent monster—they are suddenly saying he is a great commander-in-chief; he did everything right. [German Chancellor Angela] Mrs. Merkel and [French] President [François] Hollande said they are full of understanding for what Trump did; which is incredible! How can heads of government who supposedly hold up democracy and human rights, who are the defenders of Western values; how can they condone something which is so blatantly illegal?

British Foreign Secretary Boris Johnson insisted that an ultimatum should be put to Russia to give up support for President Assad; which naturally and predictably, President Putin refused.

There are many people who are warning that if Trump gets lured further into a direct conflict with Russia, that will lead to nuclear war. We are still, despite the effect of Tillerson's mission, on red alert.

What is going on? After Congressman Nunes had been shown evidence, in the Old Executive Office Building, that there was invasive electronic surveillance of Trump and the Trump team, two former high-ranking intelligence officials wrote an article with the headline "The Surveillance State behind Russia-Gate." They were Ray McGovern and Bill Binney. They said the fact that this evidence about this surveillance has now been documented, presents Trump with "the unwelcome but unavoidable choice to either confront those who have kept him in the dark about such rogue activities or live fearfully in their shadow," and capitulate to them.

Now, this is hopefully not yet a finished question, but Trump's choice of what he will do in the future, will decide whether there *is* a future for this constitutional republic, if the human species exists or not. Now earlier in the year, in the *The Bulletin of the Atomic Scientists,* they wrote that already with 90% of the world nuclear weapons at the ready in the United States and Russia, that in 2017, tensions could lead to a thermonuclear conflagration, that it is two and a half minutes to midnight, the clock is ticking. And after the U.S. military attack, Russian Prime Minister [Dmitry] Medvedev said the relationship between the United States and Russia is now completely ruined, the U.S. is on the verge of a military clash with Russia.

This was a little bit toned down, but President Trump said yesterday that the meeting with Tillerson in Moscow went better than expected, but the relationship with Russia is still very bad.

What happened to that Donald Trump who won the

election on the basis of promising to improve relations with Russia, to collaborate with Russia, to defeat ISIS, and to end the policy of regime change and interventionist wars? All these policies mentioned by Trump represent a direct threat to the British Empire. People are completely mistaken to think that the British Empire no longer exists. What happened is that after the collapse of the Soviet Union, the efforts went under way by Great Britain and the neo-cons in the United States to establish a unipolar world. One can also say it's the same thing as globalization: it's an attempt to establish a world empire based on the Anglo-American relationship; Francis Fukuyama prematurely declared the end of history, meaning the whole world would be turned into democratic states, and they came up with such things as the "right to protect," "humanitarian intervention," "regime change"—color revolution against any government that would not submit.

Enter the British Empire

And just for the record, the Ukraine crisis was *entirely* the fault of the West. It was not the fault of Russia, because when the European Union (EU) tried to bring Ukraine into the EU Association Agreement, and President Yanukovych refused that, that is what triggered the Maidan which was financed by NGOs [non-governmental organizations], by [Assistant Secretary of State] Victoria Nuland, and by people who are clearly fascists, in the tradition of Stepan Bandera. They made a coup, and Russia reacted to each step, including the situation in Ukraine, and including the vote in Crimea, which was not an annexation, but a vote of the people of Crimea that they wanted to be, again, with Russia.

The narrative about Ukraine has to be straightened out, and I would urge all of you: help us to disseminate the documentation we have made about this case. Because this is the cause for the demonization of Putin and Russia in general.

Now, this idea of regime change is what led to the Orange Revolution of 2004 earlier in Ukraine, to the Rose Revolution [in Georgia], and to the attempted White Revolution against Russia. They attempted a Yellow Revolution against China with the yellow umbrellas in Hong Kong, which fortunately, didn't go anywhere. But this was the basis for the regime change policy in Iraq, Libya, and Syria. It left much of Southwest Asia in ruins. It is the cause for the refugee crisis. It had a military side, turning the Middle East into a Hell; it had an economic side, which made the rich richer by deregulation of the banks, and made the poorer. It was the rejection of this policy paradigm which was the reason for the Brexit, which was the reason for the election of Trump, and the reason for the "No" of the Italians to the referendum by then Prime Minister Matteo Renzi—and it will continue if the injustice which is associated with that paradigm is not cured. And because we have a couple of very important elections in Europe still to come, you may have some more surprises along these lines.

It was that empire, not a nation, not Great Britain, but the idea that you can run the world as an empire by an oligarchy, which regarded the Trump election and the Trump campaign promise as an existential threat. This is why immediately after Trump was elected, the British paper *Spectator* openly said that he will not stay in office for long, he will be removed, either by assassination, impeachment, or a coup d'état.

And the role of British intelligence in creating the "dodgy dossier" by Christopher Steele, a former MI6 agent, is also very clear. And the entire story that Trump won the election because of Russian interference comes not only from the Hillary Clinton campaign, but this was concocted with the help of British intelligence.

President Putin correctly said what happened against Trump is a color revolution, is a Maidan, and that anti-Russian hysteria, targeting one of the more efficient members of the Trump administration, General [Michael] Flynn, and then [Attorney General Jeff] Sessions—this all created a McCarthyite hysteria, where just talking to a Russian diplomat is already something which makes you a stooge, an agent. It is the business of diplomats to reach out to the people of the country where they are and have contact! So the mainstream media are completely uniform in lockstep and they are continuously putting out fake news to control the narrative.

On the other side, when President Trump did something really beautiful and good, like making a speech in his Weekly Address about renewing the space program, using beautiful pictures from the Hubble Telescope, or saying he wants to revive the American System of economy, quoting Alexander Hamilton, Henry Clay, and [President Abraham] Lincoln, there was not one word in the mainstream media.

The big question is, can this coup be reversed? Well, it requires a comprehensive national and international effort. First of all, we have to mobilize Trump's base, who must understand that what is happening is a British operation. If they are just disappointed and turn away, this is not good enough, because then the efforts to control Trump will escalate and the danger is small attacks

China's New Silk Road
The Belt and Road Initative
First steps towards the World Land-Bridge

against Syria, a clash with Russia—who knows what will happen in the North Korea crisis, which is extremely hot and may get hot toward the weekend.

Remember that the American War of Independence, that which created the United States, was made against the British Empire, and the British Empire never gave up the idea of reconquering the United States. The first time they attempted that was in the War of 1812; then the British Empire allied with the Confederacy. If you go to the battlefield of Gettysburg, you can actually see the traces of this, and if you study this matter, the British banks financed the Confederacy in this war through their affiliates in Boston and Philadelphia and so forth.

Britain's War on America

The British Empire got totally upset when Trump announced that he wants to go back to the American System of economy, of Alexander Hamilton, Henry Clay, and Lincoln. You should just re-read what Henry C. Carey wrote about the difference between the British Empire economy, which makes people poor, and the American System of economy, which is concerned about the well-being of the labor force, and raising living standards and so forth.

We need people to become conscious of American history again. We need an immediate UN investigation into these chemical substances. We should distribute

the work of the former intelligence people who are already on the move, issuing open letters to President Trump trying to correct this story. The fight for Glass-Steagall must be accelerated; the bills in the House and the Senate must win overwhelming support.

Then, we should push and mobilize for President Trump, who accepted an invitation to China for early this year at his meeting with President Xi Jinping, should accelerate that visit, so that Trump should actually participate in the next month's meeting: On the 14 and 15th of May, there will be an historic summit, the Belt and Road Forum. This will be the confirmation of the New Silk Road initiative, in which already about 20 presidents of countries, 150 leaders of international organizations, and 1,200 scientists, economists, and businessmen, have agreed to participate and discuss further how to develop the idea of the Belt and Road Initiative.

This means four weeks to escalate the mobilization in the United States, for the United States to join the Silk Road.

Now, this initiative, which was announced three and half years ago by President Xi Jinping, has in the meantime developed a gigantic dynamic. It's the biggest infrastructure program in history. It's already 12 times bigger than the Marshall Plan; it already involves 70 nations and 30 international organizations. And it includes six economic development corridors and the

21st Century Maritime Silk Road. The first such corridor is the one from China to Central Asia and West Asia, going potentially into Afghanistan. When President Xi was in Iran last year, President [Hassan] Rouhani already agreed Iran will cooperate. It can be extended to Iraq, Syria, Turkey, Egypt, and Europe.

One of the next corridors is China-Myanmar-Bangladesh-India, which is right now a little bit in trouble, because India is not yet totally convinced, because they are still are a little bit in the old geopolitical view; but it would mean the first express highway between China and India.

You have the China-Western Europe route, which is developing incredibly quickly. It goes from Chengdu, Chongqing, Yiwu, and Lianyungang, to Duisburg, Hamburg, Rotterdam, Lyon, and Madrid, and it reduces the travel time of cargo and people from five weeks by ocean to two weeks by land. And it already has eight routes, and there is now a daily train leaving Chongqing to Western Europe.

Then you have the Mongolia-China-Russia corridor, which involves 32 projects. You have the China-Pakistan corridor which is huge: It is already creating 700,000 jobs in Pakistan, and it produces 10,400 kW electric power; China has invested $46 billion into that corridor.

This great project is developing great attraction, because it offers "win-win cooperation" to do what China did in the last 30 years, when they brought about the biggest economic miracle in history, by lifting 800 million people out of poverty—and the countries which are now cooperating simply will have the same advantages.

In Eastern Europe and Africa

For example: The 16 plus 1 group—these are the Central and Eastern European countries which officially are mostly in the European Union, but because the European Union has an insane austerity policy and is not investing in infrastructure, many of the East European countries are now with the New Silk Road, including Greece, Serbia, and Hungary. The EU opposes a fast train connection between Budapest and Belgrade, which is completely crazy because China is financing it, and Serbia is so happy that for the first time they are getting real investment in infrastructure. [Serbian]

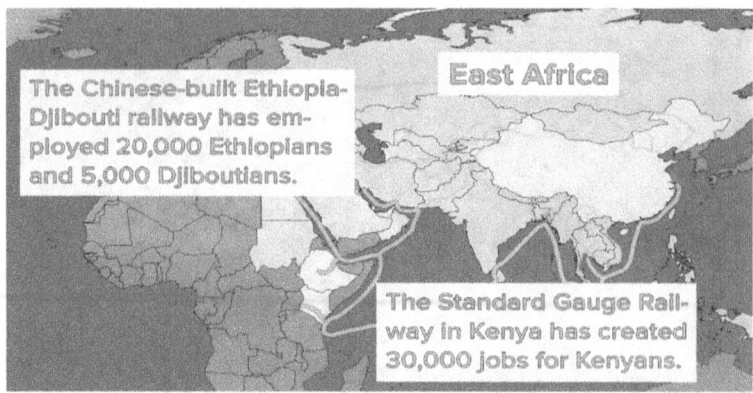

The Chinese-built Ethiopia-Djibouti railway has employed 20,000 Ethiopians and 5,000 Djiboutians.

East Africa

The Standard Gauge Railway in Kenya has created 30,000 jobs for Kenyans.

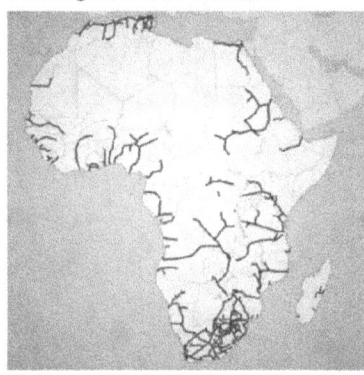
Existing Railroads in Africa

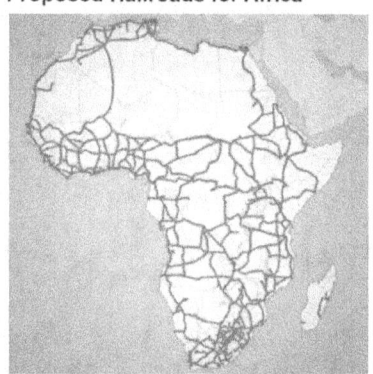
Proposed Railroads for Africa

President [Tomislav] Nikolic, who was just on a state visit to China, said that Chinese help in building their infrastructure shows the greatness of China, because they have done something which no other country did for Serbia.

But also the Swiss are absolutely happy about the cooperation with the New Silk Road. The Swiss President will go to the Beijing forum; also Italy, which has a huge problem with the refugees, as well as Spain and Portugal.

But the truly fantastic development is the change the New Silk Road is causing in Africa. There is a completely new spirit, where African leaders who for many years were completely desperate about poverty, famine, and wars, are now saying there is a real chance to overcome poverty and underdevelopment with the help of China. Just a couple of weeks ago, the first railway between Djibouti and Addis Ababa was opened. This is extremely important, if you want to transport, for example, food to these famine-stricken areas. Also, a new railway is being built between Rwanda and Congo. China is the leading job creator in Africa—they have created 30,000 jobs in the past two years, and 40,000 Africans will be trained in China. China-Africa coop-

The Transaqua Project

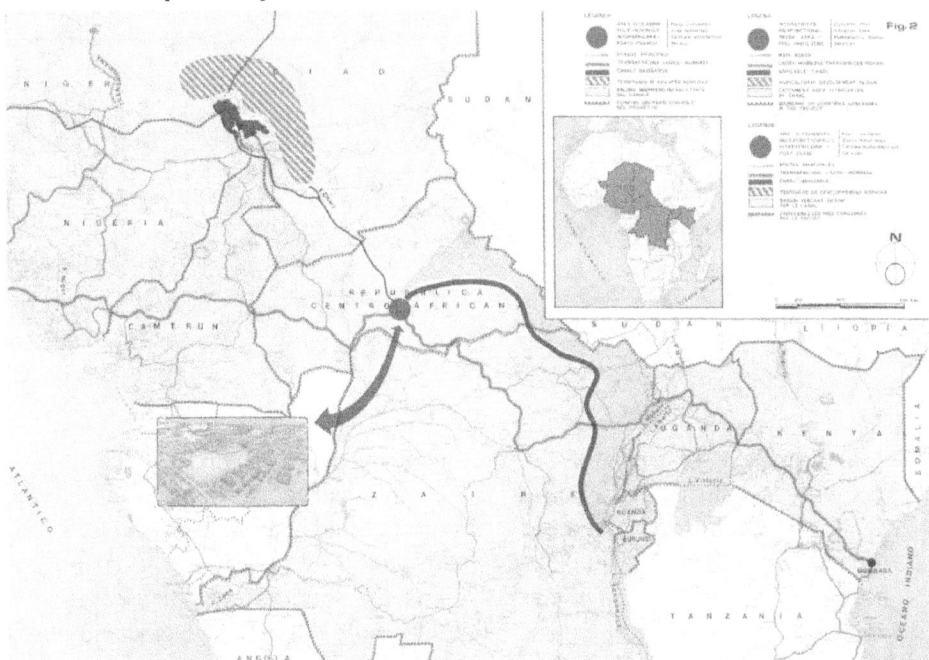

eration has been upgraded from a trade relationship, into an industrial relationship focusing on manufacturing, energy, and maritime economic development. And many Africans have told me and others that they see in the Belt and Road Initiative the possibility to realize the African Dream of poverty reduction and elimination.

China has pledged $75 billion of funding to Africa, especially for small and medium-size enterprises (SMEs). The Rwanda situation is a showcase for the Chinese model of assisting African growth. Rwanda, as you know, was struck by terrible genocide in 1994, but with the help of China it is now on a completely new path, becoming one of the fastest-growing economic areas in Africa. It's landlocked, it has almost no raw materials, but the Chinese are training the local population. They are already building the Rwanda segment of a 2,000-km northern corridor between Kigali, Rwanda, and Mombasa, Kenya, via Uganda.

The Chinese Export-Import Bank is giving a $1.2 billion loan to fund the Rwanda section which starts this year. This means that for the first time, there will be a railroad from the coast to the heart of Africa, something the colonialists never did.

Look at the slide of the Transaqua project again. This is one of the most promising projects for the future of Africa, the Transaqua Project for which we in the Schiller Institute have fought for 30 years: It's the idea

of taking the water from the tributary rivers of the Congo, at a height of 500 meters, and bringing it back through a system of rivers and canals to Lake Chad, to refill it, and it would help 12 countries to get irrigation and hydropower, and have modern navigation for shipment by water.

Now, given the starvation crisis going on in South Sudan; Somalia, where 8 million people are in danger; and in Yemen, where half the population is about to die because of the Saudi blockade, China has said that because of the refugee crisis in West Asia and North Africa, it is now the time for China to expand its humanitarian assistance and more deeply engage in global refugee governance. That since the Western countries decided to decrease contributions to the refugee crisis, and in the United States, even impose a travel ban on some people from these countries, China, given its increasing strength, will play a bigger role to help to solve this problem.

Now, if you compare that with the despicable policy of the European Union, which knows nothing better

The Western countries have decreased their contributions to accommodating the refugees, and the United States has even imposed a travel ban. China, given its increasing strength, will play a bigger role in helping to solve this problem.

than to build fences, get the EU border patrol Frontex to push people back, and to have intern camps in Turkey. They tried to do it in Egypt and Tunisia, but, fortunately, the Presidents did not go along with that. You can see that the way to go is, that if the United States, and hopefully some European countries, would join hands with Russia and with China, we can rebuild the Middle East from its war-torn condition, we can overcome poverty in Africa, and solve the refugee crisis in a human way.

In terms of investment volume, China is first in railways, but people don't know that Africa right now has the highest growth rate in new railway construction, due to Chinese investment. The Japanese monthly *Sentaku* attributed the miraculous growth in Africa to the Belt and Road Initiative, connecting the ancient trade routes in China to Europe and to Africa. The five biggest railway projects are currently being built in Africa with Chinese participation, and Chinese investment is huge! They invested $75 billion in 1,700 projects between 2000 and 2011; it has gone up since then, and in 2016 alone, they invested another $75 billion.

U.S. Participation

Now, why am I saying that the well-being, Happiness, and likely existence of mankind depends on the United States accepting the offer by Xi Jinping to join the Belt and Road Initiative? Because if the United States would leave geopolitics and cooperate in a "win-win" mode, it reverses and eliminates the danger of a geopolitical confrontation. And there are many, many areas of possible cooperation, bilateral but also involving third parties.

Now, Trump has promised to invest $1 trillion in the reconstruction of U.S. infrastructure. The American Society of Civil Engineers has said the requirements are actually $4.5 trillion, and at a recent conference in Hong Kong, some Chinese scholars made the point that the actual need is $8 trillion. Now, having driven by car yesterday from Washington to New

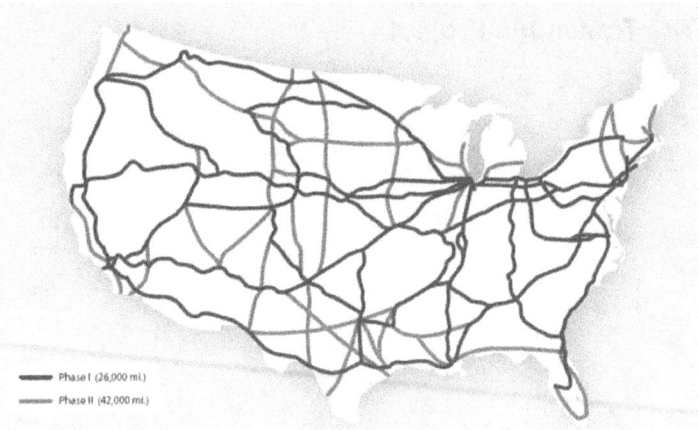

Phase I (26,000 mi.)
Phase II (42,000 mi.)

York, I would say the need is $20 trillion at least!

So, the Belt and Road cooperation could use the Chinese experience to build up U.S. infrastructure. And China has done miracles—if you go to China and you go on the fast trains, they go 350 kph, they are smooth, no noise, they don't rattle, and China has already built 20,000 km of such high-speed railways, and they want to have, by the year 2025, some 50,000 km of high-speed trains connecting all the major cities of China. But this would also be a big boost to U.S. manufacturing: It would create jobs and revitalize the U.S. economy. Because of the outsourcing under the previous free trade agreements, the United States has no more middle-level industry. They don't have a complete upstream and downstream industrial chain. China, on the other hand, has a complete industrial chain, and a relatively low cost of production. China is also the second-largest holder of U.S. Treasury bonds, and these bonds have been offered by China already to be used for infrastructure financing in the United States. My husband, Lyndon LaRouche, has long made a proposal to create a National Bank in the tradition of Alexander Hamil-

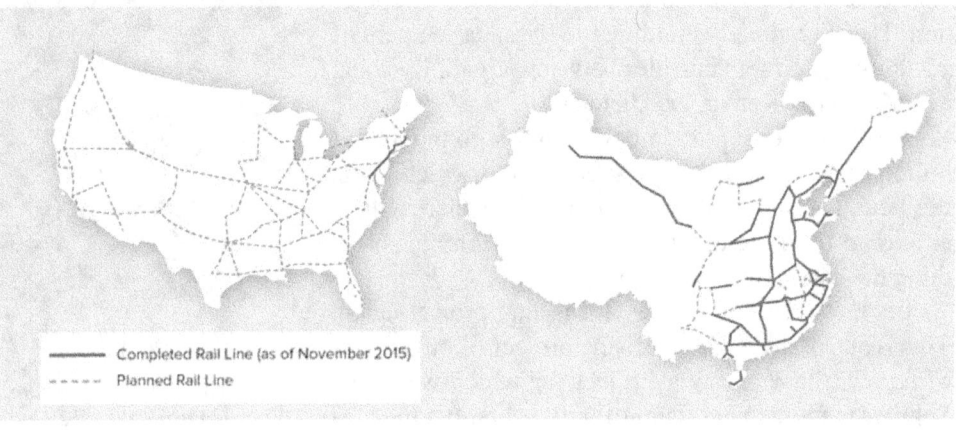

Completed Rail Line (as of November 2015)
Planned Rail Line

"The Ideal City" (ca. 1470) by the Renaissance genius, Piero della Francesca.

ton—whom Trump recently has talked about based on the American System. This National Bank could become a vehicle to move those Chinese holdings into productive investments in the United States.

So, what the United States needs, both in terms of experience in infrastructure-building, but also in terms of financing, China could provide. And I think that this kind of financing will be important, because many people who want to make 25% per year, will hesitate to invest in infrastructure, because infrastructure does not yield a direct profit, but it creates the environment for the economy to grow.

Also, a point which I think needs to be discussed much more, is that the American model of economy is actually much closer to what China is doing than people know, and since we have a day to discuss these matters tomorrow, this will also become clearer.

Now, building up U.S. industry would mean the United States can export more to China. China has a growing middle class, and because of the structural reforms initiated by President Xi Jinping, they want to build up their domestic market, which means potentially a huge market for U.S. exports. But the United States and China could also join hands and have joint ventures in third markets. The United States has more experience in investment in some countries, and then China and the United States could be complementary in their efforts. In 2016, the bilateral trade volume was $519.6 billion. The bilateral investment grew to $170 billion in the same year, but in the past 10 years, U.S. exports to China grew 11%, but Chinese exports to the United States only grew 5.6%.

Now, with the Belt and Road, this potential would

rise tremendously. If the United States, which has right now almost no train system worth speaking of, were to have such a system of infrastructure development, you could solve all problems; you could revitalize the Rust Belt; you could reindustrialize Detroit; you could have water management systems along the West Coast; and you can build beautiful new cities. This is the model of a Renaissance city, and when we build new cities, they must not look like Houston. They can be based on the Golden Mean in architecture; they can be beautiful, and they can become research centers, science cities where international scientists work together, and where students are being educated.

History of Human Evolution

When we designed the World Land-Bridge, which is actually the product of 26 years of work by the Schiller Institute—it's really a plan for the reconstruction of the world economy; it's the idea that you will have fast train systems connecting the southern tip of Latin America, Argentina and Chile; you go up by a fast train system through Central America, through North America, and connect through the Bering Strait to the Eurasian transport system; and we can really move to bigger things in the future.

If you reflect on how much mankind has progressed in the past 10-20,000 years, which on the scale of universal history is a very, very short moment: You had the first human infrastructure development when people settled by the rivers and the oceans; then they started to build roads going inland; then you had shipping, then people started to build canals—the first one in Europe promoting this idea was Charlemagne. And a gigantic

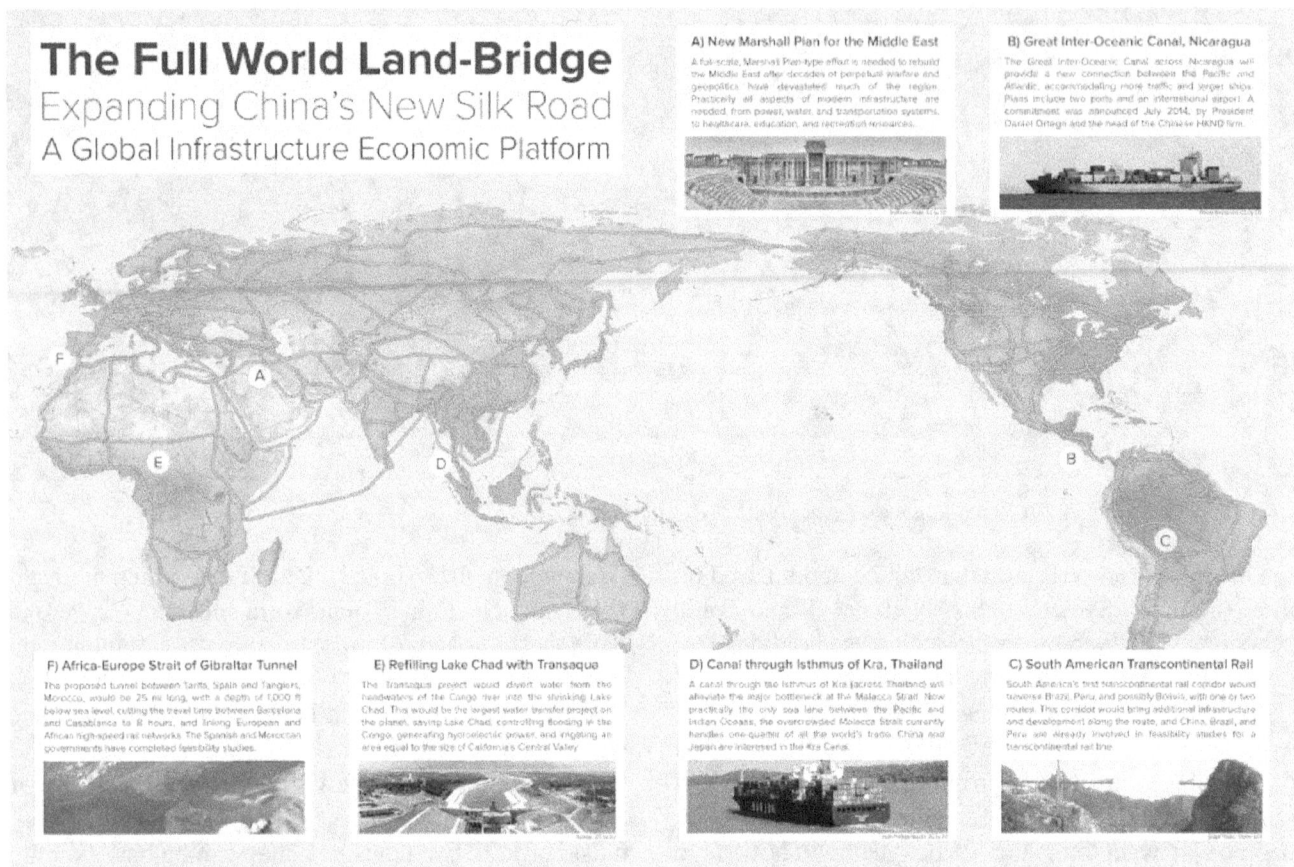

The Full World Land-Bridge
Expanding China's New Silk Road
A Global Infrastructure Economic Platform

A) New Marshall Plan for the Middle East

A full-scale, Marshall Plan-type effort is needed to rebuild the Middle East after decades of perpetual warfare and geopolitics have devastated much of the region. Practically all aspects of modern infrastructure are needed, from power, water, and transportation systems, to healthcare, education, and recreation resources.

B) Great Inter-Oceanic Canal, Nicaragua

The Great Inter-Oceanic Canal across Nicaragua will provide a new connection between the Pacific and Atlantic, accommodating more traffic and larger ships. Plans include two ports and an international airport. A commitment was announced July 2014, by President Daniel Ortega and the head of the Chinese HKND firm.

F) Africa-Europe Strait of Gibraltar Tunnel

The proposed tunnel between Tarifa, Spain and Tangiers, Morocco, would be 25 mi long, with a depth of 1,000 ft below sea level, cutting the travel time between Barcelona and Casablanca to 8 hours, and linking European and African high-speed rail networks. The Spanish and Moroccan governments have completed feasibility studies.

E) Refilling Lake Chad with Transaqua

The Transaqua project would divert water from the headwaters of the Congo river into the shrinking Lake Chad. This would be the largest water transfer project on the planet, saving Lake Chad, controlling flooding in the Congo, generating hydroelectric power, and irrigating an area equal to the size of California's Central Valley.

D) Canal through Isthmus of Kra, Thailand

A canal through the Isthmus of Kra (across Thailand) will alleviate the major bottleneck at the Malacca Strait. Now practically the only sea lane between the Pacific and Indian Oceans, the overcrowded Malacca Strait currently handles one-quarter of all the world's trade. China and Japan are interested in the Kra Canal.

C) South American Transcontinental Rail

South America's first transcontinental rail corridor would traverse Brazil, Peru, and possibly Bolivia, with one or two routes. This corridor would bring additional infrastructure and development along the route, and China, Brazil, and Peru are already involved in feasibility studies for a transcontinental rail line.

jump in human development was made with the railway system. You had transcontinental corridors, and that process will grow into the World Land-Bridge, where you will have a connection between all continents through tunnels and bridges. You will have future generations of maglev systems going through evacuated tubes where you can travel at Mach 1 very quickly to anywhere in the world. This will completely change the character of civilization.

And the next phase of human development, which already has started, is the industrialization of space, beginning with the Moon, and with fusion technology, we will soon have interplanetary travel. This will change and improve the character of our species again and again, because human beings are limitlessly perfectible. Just think about the incredible upward development of the past 10,000 years, and then think what we will do in 10,000 years from now? And that exponential development we can only have as a hypothesis.

Should we ruin this optimistic vision of the future by having a nuclear war, which will end civilization? On the sidelines of the annual National People's Congress in Beijing, Chinese Foreign Minister Wang Yi stressed the importance of China, the United States, and

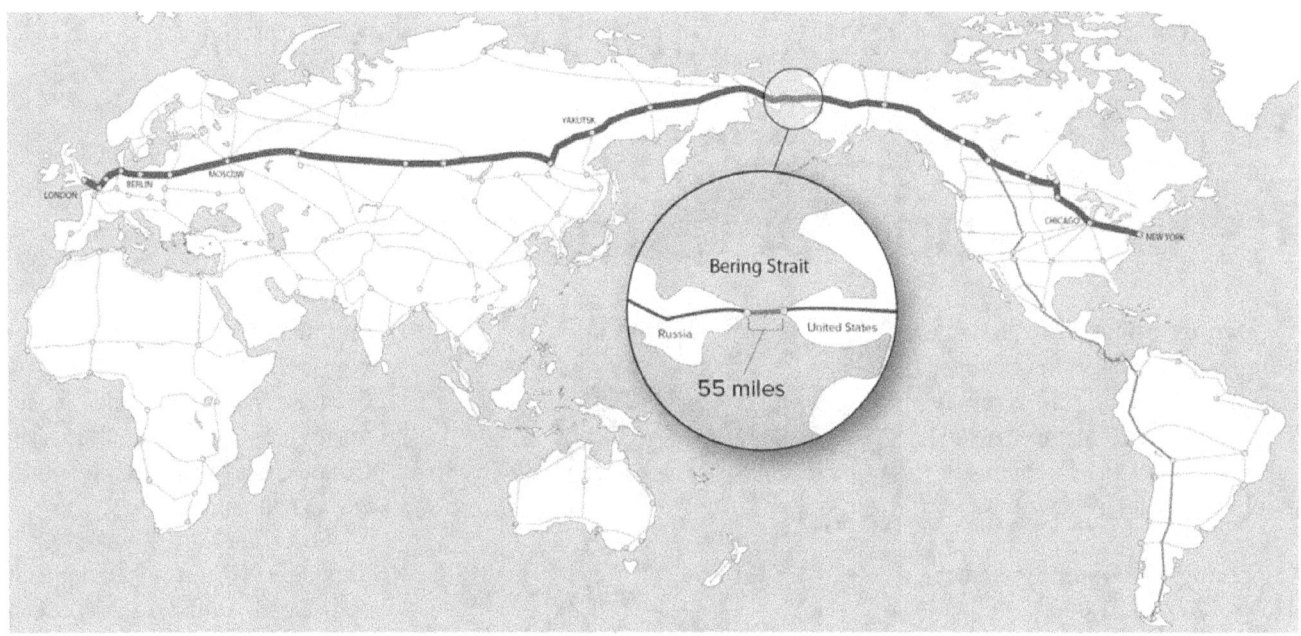

Russia working together, by emphasizing that it is the relation among these three that makes the difference. It must not be a see-saw game, not a zero-sum outcome, but their healthy collaboration means their joint responsibility for world peace.

The President of the United Nations General Assembly, Peter Thomson, recently said that the Chinese initiative of the New Silk Road/Belt and Road Initiative is the only future for mankind. And I fully agree. Because it elevates the collaboration among nations to a higher level of reason, to what Nicholas of Cusa would call "the coincidence of opposites," where the One has a higher existence than the Many. And it must be accompanied by a dialogue of the best traditions of the cultures of all nations of this world—and that will be the subject for tomorrow.

But I want to remind people that one of the founding fathers, if not *the* founding father of America, Benjamin Frank-

The Great Confucius Statue at Hermann Park in downtown Houston.

lin, discovered at a certain point the writings of Confucius, and he was so excited about Confucian teaching that he wrote that only through self-improvement can you progress and have peace, in the family, in the state, and finally, among the nations. He used the moral teachings of Confucius to shape the becoming of the United States. And the most important thing about Confucian teaching, is the idea that you must have one thing above everything else, and that is, love for mankind.

Now, Confucius said, you can love at will—if you decide to love, you can do it instantly. I think this is what we should keep in mind and have that love for mankind right now, because I think mankind is the most beautiful thing in the world, and it's in mortal danger. But the horizon, what mankind can become if we go to a new epoch, the New Paradigm of working together, and of developing each other's creativity, is limitless. So let's mobilize such a love.

How Beijing Sees Its Belt and Road Initiative

Dennis Speed: Thank you, Helga. Our next speaker is Mme. Zhang Meifang, the Deputy Consul General, at the Consulate General of the People's Republic of China in New York.

Zhang Meifang: Madame Helga Zepp-LaRouche, chairperson of the Schiller Institute, distinguished guests, ladies and gentlemen, good morning to you all. It is truly a great honor and pleasure for me to be invited to attend this morning's conference, named, "China-U.S. Cooperation on the Belt and Road Initiative and Its Corresponding Ideas in Chinese and Western Philosophy."

EIRNS
Zhang Meifang

Please, first of all, let me extend on behalf of the Chinese Consulate General in New York City, on behalf of the Consul General, Ambassador Zhang Qiyue, our heartfelt greetings to you all, and may we also wish this morning's conference to be held with full success.

And thank you so much, Mme. Helga Zepp-LaRouche, for your very interesting and very important speech, which really inspired us all. And as I understand this morning, I'm being invited to share with you what kind of meanings and characteristics does the Belt and Road Initiative carry, and what can it bring to relevant regions and other parts of the world. So perhaps these are the main topics which I'm going to share with you this morning.

First of all, let me start with what really is the initiative of the One Belt, One Road. How did it come into being? The Belt and Road Initiative is a very crucial component of China's new opening-up policy. In 2013, when President Xi Jinping made a trip to the Eastern European countries, he raised the initiative of jointly building the Silk Road Economic Belt and also, the 21st Century Maritime Silk Road, during his trip to countries in Central Asia as well as the Southeast Asian nations.

So, some three years after President Xi's proposal, the Belt and Road Initiative has been built from scratch, and now it has really taken root and bloomed in more and more countries, and won several positive responses from the international community as well. For instance, so far, about 100 countries and international organizations have already expressed their interest and also expressed their support for the One Belt, One Road initiative. Apart from this, 40 countries and international organizations have already signed the cooperation agreements.

On this point, I would like to talk about three major points, regarding the Belt and Road Initiative. First of all, the Belt and Road Initiative is a cooperative proposal based on the principle of mutual negotiation, joint development, and sharing. The history of the Belt and Road Initiative is as follows: It was as early as 2100 years ago, when Zhang Qian—probably most of you know of Zhang Qian, the Chinese explorer and diplomat at that time from the Han Dynasty—was dispatched to visit the western regions twice, and also to open up the door for friendship between China and the countries to China's west. So this everlasting and also ever-changing trade route gradually expanded, and gradually became what we call the Silk Road.

Fast forward from that time, in the Song Dynasty and also Ming Dynasty, we have another legendary figure who was named Zheng He. Zheng He commanded several expeditionary voyages down the sea to the west. So, thanks to the advanced navigation technology of that time, our ancestors successfully embarked on the Maritime Silk Road. For thousands of years, the Silk Roads have not only brought goods such as silk, parsley, and spices, but also brought peace, friendship and real benefits to the people from numerous countries around the world.

Actually, the most important historical legacy of the Silk Road is the Silk Road spirit, which is enshrined in the peace and cooperation, openness and inclusiveness, mutual learning, and also mutual benefit. Today, China's Silk Road Initiative is not only the inheritance and innovation of the ancient Silk Road, but the common aspirations of the countries along the Belt and Road to extend their mutually beneficial cooperation. Such an initiative really stands for the principle of mutual negotiation, joint development, and sharing, in order to promote policy coordination; facilitate connectivity; and increase trade, financial integration, and people-to-people bonds. The initiative also aims to promote the integration of the development strategies of the countries along the Belt and Road Initiative to enable all countries involved to complement one another, to narrow regional disparities, and to accelerate the process of the regional integration in order to raise the overall economic development of the region.

The Belt and Road Initiative is by far the most important public project China has provided to the world, and also a crucial practice for China's establishment of partnerships in the world.

Role of Chinese Tradition

As I mentioned, and probably as you know, since the establishment of this initiative three years ago, it has continuously expanded in influence, and received, as I mentioned, positive responses and support from more than 100 countries in the world, and also from international organizations. The support and engagement of all countries along the Road and the Belt and Road Initiative, has progressed smoothly and reaped an early harvest. For instance, Chinese enterprises have established more than 56 economic and trade cooperation zones in more than 20 countries along the Belt and Road, with a total investment of more $18.5 billion, and a series of major projects have been launched and flourished, stimulating the economic growth of countries along the roads, and creating many employment opportunities.

And I also want to mention in particular, that starting this January, the China-Europe freight train—as Mme. LaRouche has already mentioned—which departs from Yiwu city in east China, has arrived in London for the first time ever. Over the 12,000-km railway line, it takes the cargo train 18 days to travel through Central Asian and European countries, through the Channel Tunnel, and eventually arrive in London, with a travel time one month shorter than shipping via sea, and at a cost one-fifth that of air freight. This intercontinental freight train service has stimulated the local import and export business, given its obvious time and cost advantage, and it has become really a showcase in the Belt and Road Initiative. This is just one example.

The second point I want to talk to you about is the cultural perspective. The Belt and Road Initiative is deeply rooted in China's rich cultural traditions. It is a pragmatic and cooperative initiative. The ancient Silk Road was a road of trade, and more importantly, a road of friendship that carried humanistic and cultural exchanges as well as promoting mutual understanding of all civilizations. During China's 5,000 years of history, we have leading philosophers, such as Lao Tzu, Confucius, and Mencius, whom Mme. LaRouche has already mentioned, who put forward ideas and thoughts. Some of the most important ones and the most famous, have been to seek common ground while putting aside differences, absorbing the excesses and discarding the dross, contributing to help others when you live a good life, and positioning oneself correctly in the world to walk the correct path. These ideas still shape contemporary Chinese people's lives.

Thanks to China's 5,000 years of history and philosophy, China is a peace-loving nation. We love peace. We love to have a peaceful world, in which we love to develop our friendly relations in cooperation with all countries around the world, including this great country, the United States.

China has become the world's second largest economy, thanks to our 38 years of reform and opening to the outside world. Last year the Chinese economy was stable and very healthy. By the end of this year, we are expecting to have a steady growth of about 6.5%. So the speed of China's economic growth has transitioned from high to a medium-high, and it is expected that within the next five years, China will import $8 trillion worth of goods, with more than $750 billion of overseas investment, while outbound tourism is estimated to reach 700 million.

Currently, China has been pushing forward structural reform, guided by a vision of what we call the five most important pillars, vis-à-vis our national economic and social development. These are: innovative, coordinated, green, open, and shared development, to achieve supply-side economic restructuring and upgrading. We are willing to share with other countries the new historical opportunities China has during the entire process of promoting regional development strategy, new organization strategy, and opening-up strategy.

The third point I want to share with you, is that the Belt and Road Initiative is characterized by openness and inclusiveness as an innovative platform of great potential. At a time when the economic outlook is uncertain and the recovery is slow in the world, and also at a time when various challenges are the backdrop, contradictions between openness and exclusiveness, economic integration and fragmentation, are further highlighted. At the opening plenary session of the 2017 annual meeting of the World Economic Forum held at Davos, this January, Chinese President Xi Jinping pointed out that we shall firmly promote an open world economy, to share opportunities and profits with other countries in a process of opening up, and to realize mutual benefits and a "win-win" situation.

We shall not retreat to the harbor whenever there are wind and waves. Otherwise, we would never be able to enter the paradise of success shared by all. We shall vigorously enhance global connectivity to achieve joint growth and common prosperity with countries all over the globe.

China and the U.S.

Today, what is of great importance, when we are gathering here to talk about the Belt and Road Initiative, is that we not only broaden the space and bring historical opportunities to deepen Sino-U.S. relations and cooperation, but also note that international cooperation under the Belt and Road Initiative will not be limited to countries along the routes, but open to all countries including the United States. For more than three years, many Western companies, including those from the United States, have been substantially involved in projects related to the Belt and Road Initiative.

As you probably know, in May this year, China will host in Beijing the Belt and Road Forum for International Cooperation, which aims to discuss ways to boost cooperation, build cooperation platforms, and share cooperation outcomes. The forum will also explore ways to address problems facing the global economy, and also regional economic problems; create fresh energy

for pursuing interconnected development; and make the Belt and Road Initiative deliver greater benefits to all the people of the countries that are involved.

And thirdly, the Belt and Road Initiative is characterized by openness and inclusiveness, and is an integrated platform of great potential. As I mentioned, at a time when the economic outlook is uncertain and recovery is very slow, at a time when there are challenges as the backdrop, contradictions between openness and exclusiveness, between economic integration and fragmentation, will further be highlighted. So what we should do in this entire process is that we need to further strengthen our efforts to promote Sino-U.S. relations. In this way we can bring our initiative into full play.

Let me spend some minutes to talk about Sino-U.S. relations. China and the United States are the world's largest developing country and the world's most developed country, so the relationship between the world's largest country and the world's most developed country is perhaps the most important and most dynamic relationship in the world. At present, China is the United States' largest trading partner; the trade volume is more than 210 times as large as it was 38 years ago. In another sense, the total bilateral trade between China and the United States in 2016 reached almost $109 billion, as against less than $2 billion in the early 1980s shortly after China established diplomatic relations with the United States.

Last year also the amount of bilateral investment between our two countries reached more than $170 billion. Besides, I want to mention in particular between our two countries, that China has more than 300,000 students who pursue advanced studies in the United States. As against less than 10,000 traveling between our two countries in one year in the early 1980s, right now, we have almost 10,000 people traveling between the two sides of the Pacific *every single day*. And every 17 minutes there is a flight, flying across the Pacific. According to the statistics on the results from the U.S. side, bilateral trade and investment between China and the United States have created more than 2.6 million job openings for the United States. The number of Chinese tourists travelling to the United States reached 2.59 million last year, in 2016, creating more than $30 billion of tourism revenue for the United States.

I could talk on and on about the specific statistics about our two countries in all aspects of life, but the development and improvement in Sino-U.S. relations cannot do without the high-level talks, as Mme. La-

Rouche already mentioned in great detail about the results of the meetings between the two heads of state last week.

And I want to conclude my speech by talking about the results of the meetings between President Xi Jinping and President Donald Trump. Last week, upon the invitation of President Donald Trump, President Xi Jinping came to Mar-a-Lago where he had important meetings that are historically significant, meetings with President Donald Trump. President Xi and his wife, Mme. Peng Liyuan, were received by President Donald Trump's family, three generations. Secretary of State Rex Tillerson of the United States went to the airport to greet our President and Madame. That really showed the great importance attached by the United States to this meeting.

Summit of Two Presidents

Last week, over the days when our President was here, the leaders of the two countries have had many important meetings, during which they had in-depth exchange of views on Sino-U.S. relationships and international and regional issues of common concern, reaching many important consensuses. Both sides believed that the meeting was rooted positively and has made many important achievements. Firstly, the meeting is aimed at strengthening mutual understanding and trust of the two heads of state. President Xi Jinping and President Donald Trump shared governance theory and introduced to each other their respective ongoing priority areas, which deepens mutual understanding and establishes a very good working relationship between the two heads of state.

President Donald Trump accepted President Xi Jinping's invitation for a state visit to China later this year. Both leaders have also agreed to keep close contacts through meetings, through calls, and through letters. The deeper the two leaders communicate with each other, the bigger the role they could play in guiding China-U.S. relations, creating the relationships' compatibility and tenacity, in boosting the world's positive expectations for their further development.

And secondly, the result of the meeting is that the meeting affirms the development, through action and principles, of China-U.S. relations. Both leaders highly applauded the historic progress of Sino-U.S. relations and agreed to promote greater development to a new starting point, so as to bring more benefits to the people of both countries and the entire world. President Xi re-iterated that cooperation is the only choice for China and the United States, and that both countries are capable of becoming good partners. He pointed out in particular, that we have a thousand reasons to make China-U.S. relations a success, and no reasons to make bilateral relations a failure. President Donald Trump noted that the United States stands ready to cooperate with China to eliminate those factors and problems affecting bilateral relations, to realize and bring about greater development of China-U.S. relations. Bilateral relations will certainly be better.

Thirdly, the meeting has also laid out priority views and mechanisms of bilateral cooperation. China and the United States agreed to promote healthy development of two-way investment and trade, as well as to advance two-way investment agreement negotiations. The two heads of state have announced establishment of four high-level dialogue mechanisms which I'm not going to repeat, as Mme. LaRouche has already mentioned them just now. These four high-level dialogue mechanisms are an important achievement from the Mar-a-Lago meeting.

In addition, the two heads of state exchanged in-depth views on international and regional issues of common concern, such as the Korean Peninsula nuclear issue, and agreed to expand cooperation on regional and international issues to contribute to the maintenance of regional and world peace, stability, and prosperity.

In summary, the meeting of our two heads of state is very important, timely, and effective, which has achieved the original goal of enhancing mutual understanding, establishing mutual trust, and reaching common consensus.

Last but not least, I want to quote President Xi as saying that China welcomes the United States to participate in cooperation within the Belt and Road framework. President Xi stressed that both countries have become each other's first, largest trading partners and both peoples have benefitted a lot from it. China is pushing forward its supply-side structural reform and continuously expanding domestic demand, and the proportion of service industry in the national economy has been constantly improved. China's economy will maintain a sound development momentum, and economic and trade cooperation between the countries enjoys broad prospects. Both countries should really seize the opportunities.

So finally, I also want to thank the Schiller Institute for inviting me. Thank you.

DR. PATRICK HO

U.S.-China Cooperation—Bridge to A New World Economic Platform

What follows is an edited transcript of the presentation given by Dr. Patrick Ho at the conference, "U.S.-China Cooperation on the Belt and Road Initiative," sponsored by the Schiller Institute and the Foundation for the Revival of Classical Culture, in New York City on April 13.

Dennis Speed: Our next speaker is a co-organizer, actually, of these affairs. He is a fierce patriot of his nation, and his American-style delivery has made him particularly, shall we say "an item" among those of us here who have gotten to know him. He is the co-author of the report, *The Belt and Road Monograph 2016.*

It's my pleasure to introduce now, Dr. Patrick Ho, Deputy Chairman and Secretary General of the China Energy Fund Committee of Hong Kong, China.

Dr. Patrick Ho: Thank you, Dennis. Mme. Zepp-LaRouche, Mme. Zhang Meifang, distinguished guests, ladies and gentlemen—it's good afternoon.

I would like to thank the Schiller Institute for inviting the China Energy Fund Committee to be a co-organizer of this event. First of all, let me introduce myself. I represent the China Energy Fund Committee. The name sounds very formidable, but it is not; we are actually a think tank that's registered in China, Hong Kong, as a nonprofit organization. We are also registered in Arlington, Virginia as a 501(c)3 public charity.

We are dedicated to addressing issues relating to the emerging positions of China. Besides being a think tank, we're also a "do" tank—we don't only think, we do things. So, when we see opportunity, we research

EIRNS
Dr. Patrick Ho

into something that we think should be implemented; we see to it that these policies or suggestions get implemented. So, we're a little different from an ordinary think tank, we're a think and do tank, as well.

So if you dim the light we can begin the slides. Ladies and gentlemen, sit back and enjoy the slide show: "U.S.-China Cooperation: Bridge to a New World Economic Platform."

A World in Change—and Crisis

We live in an increasingly thriving world with hundreds of millions having been lifted out of poverty. Human ingenuity, technological advancement, and open markets have given us a world of increasing abundance. Our remarkable gains in increasing prosperity have assured us that there are in fact enough resources to go around for all of us, including our children.

Looking around the world today, however, we must acknowledge serious challenges: despite the impressive economic growth of recent decades, 1.2 billion people still live in extreme poverty. As many as 2.8 billion people lack access to modern energy services, and 800 million people remain chronically undernourished. Hundreds of millions have no access to a regular clean water supply, while billions live without basic sanitation facilities.

In 2013, the top eighty-five multi-billionaires had amassed wealth equivalent to the poorest half of the world's population of 3.5 billion people. The top ten percent of earners have fared exceedingly well, while

Serious Challenges in the Globe

Globalization 1.0: A System in Crisis

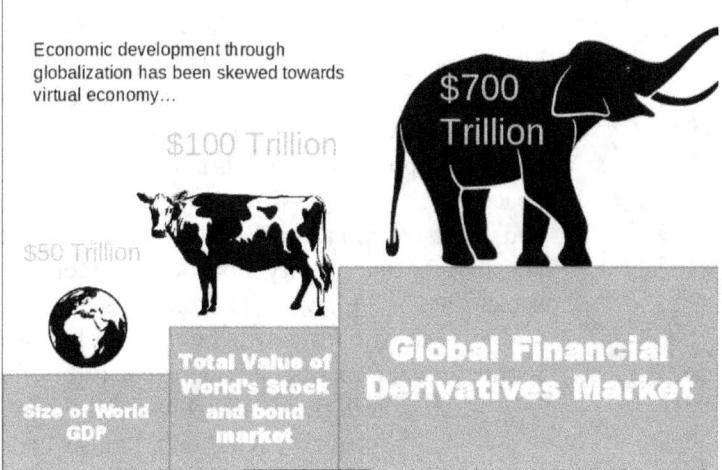

the bottom ten percent have continued to fall further behind. These trends repeat themselves not just globally, but also within nations and within cities. Even where there is healthy GDP growth, wealth accumulates primarily at the top. In the United States, despite a doubling of GDP over the last thirty years, income for the low-skilled workers has remained stagnant.

The pie has become bigger, but proportioned increasingly unfairly, across the globe, across generations, and within nations, resulting in real and significant consequences: Those who have been left behind, finding no recourse to address systemic unfairness in society, resort to extreme measures such as violence and terrorism to make their voices heard. Ultimately, everyone is harmed by inequality.

What are the origins of these challenges, and how

can they be addressed? Such tragic results can be traced back to the broken system of economic development.

Since the last millennium, the world's international order has been largely dictated by the disposition of natural resources. Many of the challenges we face today still stem from the zero-sum game of capturing resources for the security and interest of individual nations. Countries, in the name of national security, seek to secure strategic commodities for their development. And this concern is only heightened when growth exceeds the local supply of available natural resources.

At this point, countries have traditionally expanded their territories overseas, looking for new markets and increased access to resources. For most of human history, this involved plundering, slaves, colonies, and wars, with some countries annexing foreign territories in the name of religion, civilization, progress, and democracy. And others regularly pillage for spoil. Empire and imperialism reign.

Thing changed after the two World Wars, when imperialism and colonialism gave way to democracy and human rights. The answer that emerged was globalization. Globalization deploys capital and investment, trade and goods, people, and services and information across national barriers, based on a model of free trade. It has proven to be a very effective scheme for amassing great fortune, and it has accelerated growth in the global economy.

Free trade, however, has also come with its share of disadvantages. Most notably, it has disproportionately benefitted the capitalist class while leaving lower skilled workers struggling to make ends meet. This inequality has not only become a source of social strife and resentment, but also a real obstacle to continued economic growth. In the developed world, workers now protest against free trade, vilifying offshore workers and foreign investments.

In the developing world, a failure to share the fruits of progress has resulted in even greater hopelessness and despair. The absence of a future to look forward to, coupled with economic and political uncertainty, has given birth to violent extremism and terrorism. Today's youth are resorting to desperate measures and joining extremist groups and organizations. In either case, the

BRI—A New Model of Connectivity

BRI—New Paradigm of Development

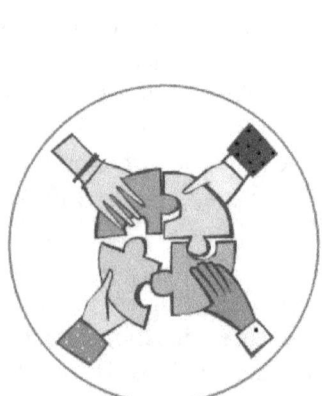

Globalization 1.0 is only concerned with maximizing profits...

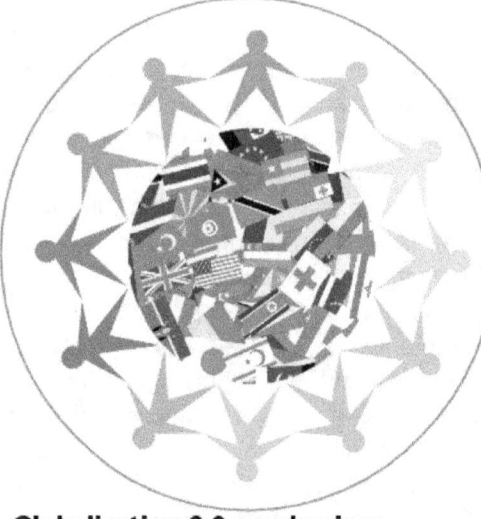

Globalization 2.0 emphasizes economic prosperity amidst equality and environmental responsibility.

end result is conflict, discord, and instability within and among nations, all of which tragically have undercut and undermined the drivers of human progress.

For the last half-century, economic development through globalization has been skewed towards the virtual economy and service industries, including financial derivatives. This has been accompanied by astronomical national debts with ever-widening income gaps, wealth disparity, instability in the financial system itself, and all its inherent social woes.

Our world is now desperately searching for a new paradigm of development, one which will return us to a policy of balanced economic development where asset-based physical and real economy, such as investment in infrastructure development, plays a central role.

Globalization 2.0

Today, Globalization 1.0 is a system in crisis. However, to return to isolationism and protectionism would be against the overall trend of human progress. The world is in dire need of Globalization 2.0. And China's Belt and Road Initiative (BRI) is the answer to this need.

If we aspire to live on this planet happily and peacefully, we must shift to a more sustainable and inclusive model of development. It is not possible for one country alone, or one sector of society alone, to have a hold on all the wealth and enjoy the fruits of prosperity. This only leads to resentment from our neighbors who rightfully seek their own path to fulfillment. Inequality leads only to insecurity and instability, ultimately harming both those who have too much and those who have too little. What we need today, instead, is a strategy for development anchored in the principle of inclusiveness and sharing. By sharing growth and security, we can ensure development that is long-lasting and sustainable. And this is the underlying spirit and intention of the Belt and Road Initiative.

Ever since the reform and opening up initiated in 1978, China has pursued rapid development by embracing the open market economy. China's accession to the World Trade Organiza-

BRI Is a Grand Vision

A policy has ....
- **Fixed** policy agenda
- **Rigid** mechanism

A Vision is ....
- **Ambitious** and **farsighted**
- **Flexible, accommodating** and **adaptable** to new conditions

tion in 2001 ushered in a spell of rocketing development. By 2015, China's GDP had multiplied sevenfold since 2000, and 184-fold since 1978. It is now the second largest economic aggregate in the world, after the United States.

But the economic prosperity of China has been paid for with a heavy toll on the environment and on income equality. With rising wages and escalating land premiums, coupled with renewed public concerns for social justice and equality, China has now reached a bottleneck in economic development, just like other maturing economies.

Facing these costs and challenges, China has realized that the current approach to economic growth, with its emphasis on profits and returns, is unsustainable. The country understands that only a new mode of growth and development will be able to address fundamental issues, such as inequality, lack of natural resources, and excess manufacturing capacities, in one go. And history is full of stories of nations that have opted for colonization or war as answers to foundering economic growth.

China will do neither. It has chosen a third pathway, a road of peaceful co-development, driven by a strategy of sharing with its neighbors, and anchored around the economic principle of "win-win" cooperation.

So, in 2013, Chinese President Xi Jinping put forward his strategic concept of building the One Belt, One Road initiative, now called the Belt and Road Initiative, or BRI. This involves constructing economic and cultural corridors along the ancient Silk Road and the maritime Silk Road. It is a grand vision of peace, development, cooperation, and a "win-win" outcome.

This vision aims to create the most promising economic corridor in the world, directly benefitting a population of 4.7 billion people—of sixty-five countries, or sixty-seven percent of the global population—mostly from the developing economies. With a collective GDP of $27 trillion, this grouping accounts for about thirty-eight percent of the world's production. Indeed, it is a grand vision for international cooperation.

The characteristics of the Belt and Road Initiative are:
- Goodwill,
- Sharing,
- Inclusiveness, and
- A People-to-People approach.

The first, **Goodwill:** The Belt and Road Initiative is all about connecting countries and peoples, accommodating differences, embracing diversity, realizing potential, and enabling various goals and prospects, fostering goodwill.

Sharing: Under the Belt and Road Initiative, if China has excess capacity and a surplus of funds, it will be shared. By helping neighbors to grow and making them into friends that are just as developed as itself, China recognizes that it, too, will in turn become more stable, more secure, and more prosperous.

Inclusiveness: The Belt and Road Initiative is open to all countries and all people interested in being connected for mutual development, regardless of form of government, cultural and religious background, or geographic location. It is guided by the desire to build communities and bring people in, to see others prosper as a seed, just as China has in recent decades.

People-to-People: This model, which promotes common experience, will ultimately lead to relationships that are meaningful and long-lasting, based on a sense of community rather than competition. In so doing, the Belt and Road Initiative addresses not only economic challenges but also cultural and social ones, promoting values of sharing and solidarity with all people. The Belt and Road Initiative provides the foundations for peace.

This initiative aims to promote the connectivity of the Eurasian continent and adjacent areas. It is expected that in the coming years, new roads and new railways will be built, new sea lanes and new flight paths opened, and oil pipelines and electric grids connected. It is a new model of connectivity among peoples.

However, connectivity is not merely building roads and bridges or making linear connections between dif-

Adopting an alternative approach to counter complex challenges.

ferent places on the surface. More important, it should be a three-dimensional combination of infrastructure, institutions, and people-to-people exchanges, and also a five-way multifaceted progress in policy communication, infrastructure connectivity, trade links, capital flows, and understanding among peoples. Simply put, the Belt and Road Initiative regards infrastructure development as providing the basic building blocks of global connectivity and social economic growth.

The Belt and Road Initiative represents a new model of sustainable development for the world, Globalization 2.0, where social inclusiveness, equality, and individual and social well-being are featured alongside economic growth and prosperity, with equal weight given to every one of them.

Prosperity is achieved through collective, inclusive approaches, built on trust, social justice, goodwill, dialogue, and collaboration among countries.

Whereas Globalization 1.0 concerns itself only in maximizing profits, Globalization 2.0 emphasizes economic prosperity amidst equality and environmental responsibility.

Infrastructure

In its formative stages, the Belt and Road Initiative will rely on making investments in infrastructure building, putting a call out to the entire world to start steering the global economy back to basic real assets and gradually away from virtual derivatives and deficit spending.

Investing in infrastructure is a proven way to invest in our future, providing a foundation and an impetus for growth and development.

The term "infrastructure," however, encompasses physical structures as well as institutions and human capabilities. Economic infrastructure includes: transportation, energy, communications, and financial services systems. Social and environmental infrastructure, however, includes water and sanitation, schools, hospitals, and healthcare systems.

Infrastructure-based economic development requires that a substantial proportion of the nation's resources must be systemically directed to its long-term assets, such as transportation and energy, as well as social infrastructure such as schools, universities and hospitals. This defines the long-term economic efficiency of stimulating growth in economically lacking regions and fostering technological innovation and social equity, while providing free education and affordable healthcare for all.

Infrastructure is an economic driver and forms the backbone of economy in every country and the necessary input to every economic output. It is critical to a nation's prosperity, public health, welfare, and human resources. The condition of infrastructure has a cascading impact on the nation's economy, business productivity, GDP, employment, personal income, and international competitiveness.

Infrastructure does not favor big enterprises only,

but also helps medium, small, and even individual enterprises to thrive and prosper, providing them with access to technology and pathways into markets. Such social empowerment creates opportunities, especially for individuals to lift themselves out of joblessness and poverty.

The United Nations' "2030 Agenda for Sustainable Development" notes that infrastructure investments in transport, irrigation, energy, information, and communication technologies are crucial to achieving sustainable development and empowering communities in many countries. It has long been recognized that growth in productivity and incomes, and improvements in health and education outcomes require investments in infrastructure.

However, there are multiple challenges in building sustainable infrastructure. First and foremost, the global infrastructure gap is a significant challenge:
• 2.6 billion people face difficulty in accessing electricity full time,
• 2.5 billion people lack access to basic sanitation,
• 800 million people lack access to water, many hundreds of millions of them in sub-Saharan Africa and South Asia,
• 1-1.5 billion people do not have access to reliable phone services.

The "Addis Ababa Action Agenda" addressed the need to bridge the infrastructure gap in developing countries, requiring an expenditure of $1-$1.5 trillion annually.

Even in many developed western nations, much of the basic infrastructure is out of date, at least a half-century old, and needs renovation, especially that in the United States. Infrastructure projects lack sufficient investment by the public and private sectors. And most big infrastructure projects run twenty months late and eighty percent over budget.

The Belt and Road Initiative is a grand vision. Unlike other regional cooperation projects, which are for a fixed policy agenda and a set mechanism similar to the Marshall Plan, the Belt and Road Initiative is a grand vision, providing infinite room for creative solutions and possibilities in implementation. The Belt and Road is ambitious and farsighted, but at the same time, also flexible, accommodating, and adaptable to new conditions and challenges. It provides an overarching theme and umbrella under which any form of cooperation can be made possible. Governments, businesses,

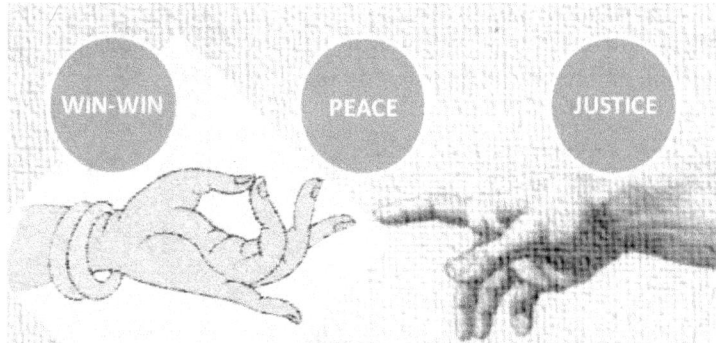

BRI helps the world to get rid of its current political, economic, and developmental crises

think tanks, and populations can contribute continuously to this initiative, as well as to new interpretations and new content, enriching its material so as to further cooperation and shared benefits.

We all have different pasts, but we also have a common future to face. The Belt and Road Initiative is a visionary strategy for sustainable growth and development that is inclusive of all mankind. This is not only for China, but a model for all countries and all peoples. Motivated by goodwill, China is inviting people and countries along the Belt and Road to build a community of shared interest and common destiny, a community where no one is left behind, and no one has to take second place.

Simply put: The Belt and Road Initiative is neither about seeking a sphere of influence, nor striving for hegemony. It is about connecting countries and peoples, accommodating differences, embracing diversities, realizing potentials, sharing capacities, and enabling various goals and prospects.

It is a positive endeavor to seek new models of international cooperation and global governance, and will inject new positive energy into world peace and development. It paves the way for building a community of common destiny for all mankind.

Promise of the BRI for the U.S.A.

When the Belt and Road Initiative was launched in 2013, we knocked on American doors, which did not open. … And today, we are banging on Mr. Trump's door, and chanting "Open, Sesame!" Ladies and gentlemen, I think after today's discussion, I must say our

"Open, Sesame!" is a big yell to the new American administration to reconsider the Belt and Road Initiative as an impetus to rethink and realign U.S. foreign policy for a new century.

I can summarize the salient points and outline the areas for the new administration's consideration as follows. These are only suggestions as ways for the U.S.A. to hop onto the bandwagon of the Belt and Road Initiative.

1. Consider using the Belt and Road Initiative as a platform to spearhead social and economic initiatives and programs conducive to a closer cooperation between countries and regions.

2. Realign trade agreements with Pacific countries and Atlantic countries, too, to accommodate the Belt and Road Initiative.

3. Urge national and regional development banks and kindred institutions to assist in financial agreements or arrangements to support infrastructure developments of the Belt and Road Initiative, especially from the private sector.

4. Cultivate an enabling environment for private and institutional funds to participate in mending the infrastructure investment gap.

5. Produce leadership in ensuring security on land and at sea for Belt and Road Initiative infrastructure and related projects.

6. Participate in the rebuilding of peace, stability, and hope in the war-torn and troubled regions of the world, through social-economic incentives derived from the BRI and projects related to the process of reconstruction of the countries that had been bombed and brought into war.

From Point 6, we see that the real merits of the Belt and Road Initiative lie in its geopolitical benefits, not just for China or those involved with this initiative, but for all countries in the world, by bringing stability, hope, and peace to our much-troubled world.

Our world is experiencing profound and complex challenges, including the rise of radicalization and violent extremism, against the backdrop of cultural and religious tensions. Countering these challenges has necessitated a wide range of approaches to promoting tolerance and reconciliation, not to mention the resources and efforts that have been devoted to combat-

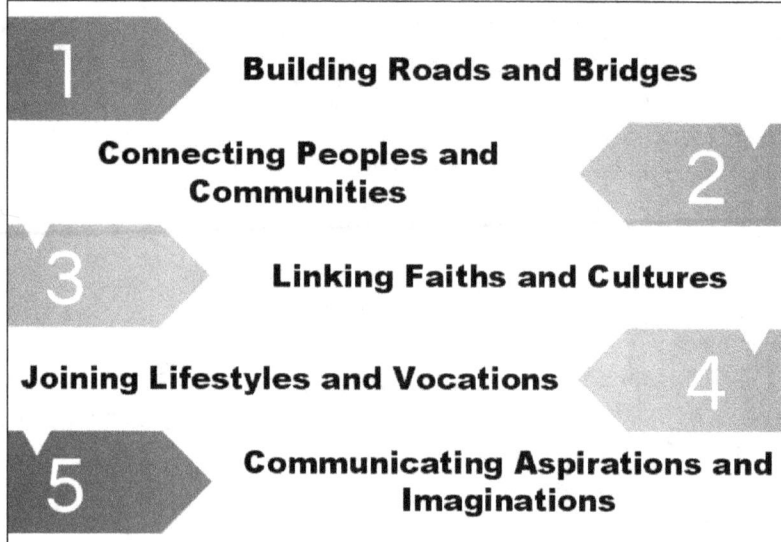

Creation of World Peace, Friendship and Prosperity

1. Building Roads and Bridges
2. Connecting Peoples and Communities
3. Linking Faiths and Cultures
4. Joining Lifestyles and Vocations
5. Communicating Aspirations and Imaginations

ing terrorism in the last decades—but all with discouraging, if not dismal results.

Perhaps we have been addressing only the symptoms without attending to the roots of the problem, and it is high time that we take a look and reconsider adopting an alternative approach.

The political problems in the Middle East and North Africa cannot be solved by military might alone. Only by changing the underlying socio-economic conditions in those regions can we provide hope and a future for the great masses of young people who today are living in despair, and resorting to desperate measures by joining these extreme formations.

The Belt and Road Initiative's many infrastructure projects would bring a massive amount of jobs, generating economic activities and addressing the employment concerns of the increasing youth population in those areas, while bringing peace, hope, and long-lost stability to the troubled regions of Middle East and North Africa, integrating them with the global economy, and helping to mitigate the social ills spawned by periodic bombings, incessant wars, and the rapidly growing wealth gap from Globalization 1.0.

The Belt and Road Initiative operates according to the geo-economic principles of "win-win cooperation" and overcomes the zero-sum game of geopolitical confrontation that threatens to bring the world close to war. The Belt and Road brings peace and justice by reducing inequalities. It has the potential to help the world to get rid of its current political, economic, and development crises.

Ladies and gentlemen:

The two previous Silk Roads traded tea, silk, spices, exotic fruit, jewelry, and gold. This 21st Century Silk Road offers an exchange of creative ideas, views and perspectives, traditions and legacies—it exchanges kindness, it offers peace!

The modern Silk Road teaches us to learn mutual respect, and to recognize that despite our different backgrounds, there are fundamental values we all hold dear, basic principles we all respect, and core understandings we all embrace. By reaching out and bringing in, we can create world peace, friendship, and prosperity.

Ultimately the Belt and Road Initiative is about building roads and bridges throughout the entire world, connecting peoples and communities, linking faiths and cultures, joining lifestyles and vocations, and communicating aspirations and imaginations in one glorious celebration of diversity of values and accommodation with harmony.

Ladies and gentlemen:

The Belt and Road Initiative is a global challenge calling for global participation. Through this initiative, China is sending out a most sincere message, loud and clear, of collaboration and partnership, to all our friends and foes from near and far, to work together to find solutions to sustainable growth for all of humanity. By sharing, we become better partners in the balancing of our prospective goals, achieving our common dreams.

A very famous Chinese, Sun Yat-sen, once had a dream. He said: "Once our goal of modernizing China is accomplished, the dawn of a new century will shine upon our beautiful country, and the whole of humanity will enjoy a more brilliant future."

And a not so famous Chinese, Patrick Ho, had a dream, too. And he said, "I have a dream. I dream of a cultural China, with ideas and values to inspire humanity. The redefinition of Chinese core values signifies the awakening of a modern humanity, and would eventually lead to another human Renaissance of our modern time."

The Belt and Road Initiative is a world bridge connecting all dreams. This dream is not only the dream of 1.3 billion Chinese, over 5,000 years. … It is also a world dream, the dream of peace on Earth and the world as one. The dreams belong to all of us. It belongs to you, and to me.

I thank you.

For a Broader Eurasian Partnership

Remarks of Pyotr Ilyichov, Chargé d'Affaires of the Permanent Mission of the Russian Federation to the United Nations, to the Schiller Institute conference in New York, April 13.

Dennis Speed: I'd like to introduce our final speaker. We're all aware of a particular circumstance that has erupted, and those of us who are real American patriots recognize that a great injustice is being done. We are opposed to that injustice, and we are very happy to have the next speaker here, and in our presence: He is Mr. Pyotr Ilyichov, Chargé d'Affaires of the Permanent Mission of the Russian Federation to the United Nations. [standing ovation]

Pyotr Ilyichov: Thank you, thank you colleagues for a very warm welcome, and I am grateful for Mme. LaRouche for organizing your conference that is very pertinent for what we're discussing. I do apologize for coming too late, but we had two meetings today at the Security Council, two major issues that are far away, but are proving that we live in a globalized world and this globalized world is moving in two directions. Sometimes we have very decent, very good consequences of globalization, sometimes we have negative effects. So today we discussed Haiti—that looks more or less on a positive trend; but again, what the President just said, that mass migration of people creates more problems, but with a geo-communitarian attention, we can try and turn this negative phenomenon into a benefit both for hosting communities, but also for those people who are traveling.

And the second issue we were discussing was Somalia and Eritrea, and you can also imagine that this is a very important topic, not only because of the plight of the Somalis that are, for more than 25 years, deprived of statehood, of truly having a nation. But they did sur-

EIRNS
Pyotr Ilyichov

vive, and unfortunately they are located in such a strategic position that it is being used by everybody—by Western powers, by bad guys, Al-Shabaab terrorists—but now there is a clear linkage to the Islamic State, and also there is piracy.

So we see that this globalized world requires also a globalized reaction, a globalized answer.

'We Are Proud of China's OBOR'

But coming back to the theme of your conference, I would like to say international economic development and cooperation nowadays are a driving force in the world that we live in. It would be true to say that one of the main objectives of each country is to develop diverse economic, scientific, and technological ties, not only between the individual countries but also between the groups of countries, and those ties, this cooperation should be based on principles of independence, equality, and mutual respect for each other's interests.

Each country has its own strategic project, and we are proud of the initiative that our Chinese colleagues put forward. They are driving to revive the historic Silk Road, and by establishing two corridors, one on land and the other by sea, they will connect Asia via Central Asia, via the Middle East, into Europe. Indeed, this phenomenon of One Belt, One Road (OBOR) is a very promising project that will boost economic cooperation, but also will affect very positively the geostrategic situation in that region.

But in addition, my country, Russia, has been developing relations with Asia-Pacific countries. Of course, our strategic partner is China: We are developing our special relations with the People's Republic of China. China is our biggest economic trade partner; it's our neighbor. We have common interests, not only in the sphere of economic policies, but also other humanitarian issues like health and cultural exchanges, and we are trying to complement each other both in the political and economic dimensions.

In fact, the cooperation that we have with China, is the cooperation of strategic partnership. Lately, our economic cooperation came to a very high level—our mutual trade reached $40 billion, and the plans are for that to come to $50 billion, and we are on the way. This strategic partnership between Russia and China is not only in the political sphere—of course we are two permanent members of the UN Security Council, and we cooperate very closely in that august body—but also, we have other organizations in which we are trying to cooperate, first of all the Shanghai Cooperation Organization, but also others, like the Asia-Europe Meeting (ASEM) and like BRICS. Russia is trying to promote the harmonization of the economic formats that are there, and this harmonization should be done on principles of transparency, and of respect for each other's interests.

A Broader Eurasian Partnership

From our side, we are trying to build the Eurasian Economic Union (EAEU), and we apply these principles to this economic format. What we are trying to do is not to just create this new union, but also to expand its ties, expand its cooperation with other economic entities that are there, and we think that this is a good opportunity, that we can try to confer privileges, favors that the EAEU can provide with this initiative of the One Belt, One Road, which the Chinese are trying to implement. In effect, we are trying to promote a broader Eurasian partnership, so that other hubs, other formative centers in the Eurasian integration area, could be brought in together.

We are starting to implement this broader agenda. We concluded an agreement with Vietnam, between the EAEU and Vietnam, in the free trade area. Now we are in negotiations with China. So, if it's right to align this initiative of One Belt, One Road with the Eurasian Economic Union, then that would be a huge incentive for creating not only Eurasian economic trade, but a space that will promote free relations of mutual understanding in this big, big space that we have. We are working not only with China and with Vietnam, but India is forthcoming, as is Pakistan, plus all the states that belong to the Commonwealth of Independent States.

President Putin has said that he is going to partici-pate in the summit on One Belt, One Road that is going to be held in China in May. Today he met with the Vice Premier of the State Council of China, and promised his participation, and promised to look very attentively and very favorably at this development initiative.

So, we look to a bright future for the One Belt, One Road, and think that your initiative is very pertinent, and with our discussion we are trying to contribute to moving it forward.

Thank you.

Russia and the United States

Speed: Sir, among us, we are people who organize for a very specific vision of the world, and you've referenced it. And obviously, your nation has not been able to directly talk to the American people. You've talked at the United Nations; you're talking to diplomats and others. But here, there's a cross-section of the American people—there are people here from many different parts of the country. And since you have an opportunity, I'd just like to ask you to deliver a message to them, as to what you think they should know about Russia and what you think they should be confident in, shall we say, about the intent of Russia toward the American people.

Ilyichov: Thank you. Thank you for this very difficult question [laughter], but I would say that we should not be afraid of each other. We should talk to each other. It's very important, and yesterday's negotiations of Secretary of State Rex Tillerson in Moscow, both with Foreign Minister Sergey Lavrov and President Vladimir Putin, proved that two major powers, the two most powerful nuclear states, gain more when we are talking, but not when we are reacting and trying to build alliances and counter-alliances against each other.

Russian policy was very clear from the very beginning: We don't want any special status in the world arena. We want equal treatment, fair treatment, not only for us, but for all other states. And if we can provide this fair treatment in all spheres, equal security, equal economic cooperation, and equal exchanges between people, we are all going to gain a lot—instead of trying to build new walls, trying to build new divides, and trying to build or rebuild or strengthen those military alliances that exist.

I don't know if I answered your question, but I will be more than happy to develop it with others. Thank you.

Speed: Thank you.

JACQUES CHEMINADE

LaRouche Associate Is Candidate For President of France

EIR editor Tony Papert interviewed Odile Mojon, Jacques Cheminade's campaign manager, on April 14.

Tony Papert: Who is Jacques Cheminade?

Odile Mojon: Jacques Cheminade is a former French official who happened to be assigned in the 1970s to New York City, where he met Lyndon LaRouche, and he shared with Lyndon LaRouche a very staunch dedication to justice: Economic justice, social justice, political justice, and I would add, also, cultural justice.

And from that point, he started to defend these ideas in France, in the same way that Lyndon LaRouche did in the United States.

Papert: He's run for President of France before—can you tell us about his previous campaigns for President?

Mojon: Yes, actually, there were three campaigns, and we tried twice in between, in 2002 and 2007, to qualify him as a candidate, but in these cases it didn't work. So, it's the third time that he's run. The first was in 1995, the second in 2012, and this year. And what was characteristic was that the first time, the opposition was extremely violent, but Cheminade was remembered by those who really interest themselves in politics, as the man who had told them that we were heading for a crisis—that a vey big crisis was coming. So he is remembered for that.

Then in 2012, this was also a very difficult cam-

Solidarité & Progrès

Presidential candidate Jacques Cheminade being interviewed in Clichy, Paris, France.

paign, but he was able to bring in certain other questions, including restoration of Glass-Steagall—the necessity to separate commercial from investment banks. Also, the need for big infrastructure projects, including projects in space—many journalists tried to ridicule him on the question of space exploration, but it's very funny, because now, in the mean time, *Curiosity* has landed on Mars and other successes have occurred in space exploration. And the people who have tried to ridicule Cheminade now appear ridiculous—a very funny thing. And it's still a debate today, but much less, because in a certain way, Cheminade won on this.

Sure, he was ridiculed, but at the same time, those people who were really thinking in depth, were obliged to recognize that he was right. That's why we have many people who think Jacques Cheminade is a visionary—a man who has a vision, who is not acting from petty calculations, or mere electoral considerations in the Presidential election—but a man who has a vision.

No to the Euro, No to Deschooling

Papert: Could you say more about Jacques Cheminade's plans for France, and his platform?

Mojon: Three things are very important on the negative side, so to speak: to get out of the euro, the European Union, and NATO. And on the political side, how do we rebuild the economy. Which means once we are out of the euro, once we are out of the European Union, we have to make sure that we have banking separation, and that money flows again into the real economy, namely great projects. But to ensure that, we primarily need to have first a national bank. We need to have contro l of the emission of currency, and a national banking institution which provides credit and ensures that it goes into specific programs.

The motto of his campaign is very simple: "Let's liberate ourselves from the financial occupation; let's get out of the cultural occupation." And that question of culture is also a very, very important aspect of his campaign, and we strongly insist on the question of culture, and also education, because in France right now, people are terribly worried about the education being given to their children. There is a deep debate, because the schools have almost been destroyed. Perhaps I wouldn't go quite that far, but what has been going on for years and years, is an attempt to really destroy the schools step by step, and now it has reached a very, very worrying situation; what has been going on is very worrying. This question of education is key.

Papert: And what does he say about education positively?

Mojon: First, we have to reinstate an education which is based on knowledge. Beginning in primary school, it is very important that children learn how to speak and to write. It seems obvious. But we have reached such a point that you have children in school who have difficulty in writing. They don't know how to write. Today in France, when children are ten years old, when they go on to high school, 25% are not able to express themselves properly in writing, or to speak properly. Often they don't have the vocabulary to be able to express ideas. It is a huge problem, because these children are the ones who will have to take charge of the country later—they will be the generation to take charge.

Occupied France Is not France

Papert: What is France's role in the world, in Jacques' view, or what should be France's role in the world?

Mojon: France has to become France again. Because when France is loyal to herself, then she is able to do positive things in the world. This means again the question of culture, and it means the question of political will. Today this political will does not exist, because France is only a prisoner of this financiers' occupation. Of course, in this new world, France is a middle-sized country, but here France has to play its role in supporting the deterrent of the weak against the strong. This is very important. But if we want to have this deterrent, it must be on principle. We cannot forget this principle, the republican principle, because France is a republic. And this is also a very strong debate now in France, actually. But if you forget that, then you cannot play this role. Basically, that's what Jacques Cheminade is trying to bring into the Presidential campaign, and that's why there are a lot of people who are listening to him.

I must add that he has been fighting very much on the question of the financial occupation, which is also a huge debate here. Because people are starting to understand that if they want to be free, if they want to be able to play a positive role in the world, they have to free themselves from this occupation.

Cheminade in Lebanon

Papert: Jacques just recently took a trip to Lebanon and met with President Michel Aoun.

Mojon: I see this trip as extremely important, because of course there is a long history between Lebanon and France. It's also important because there is so much disinformation concerning all the crises in the Middle East, that it was very, very important to let the people of France know what the real situation is there, and to remind them of it. Another question very much debated in France is the question of immigration. And it's very important for people to understand that if you take the case of Lebanon, it's a tiny country, where 25% or even more are refugees, mostly from Syria and Palestine. It's very important to face the role of France—the very unfortunate role—in being complicit in what has been going on in the Middle East.

And I think it's also very important for the Lebanese people living in France, or Franco-Lebanese people, that there is someone saying that it is impossible to think there is going to be peace if there is no mutual economic development. This is something which has been widely discussed.

Solidarité & Progrès

Interview with Jacques Cheminade during a visit to farm of a rural cooperative in the Retz countryside.

Surprise in the Televised Debate

Papert: Jacques was in the national television debate as one of the eleven candidates last week. What can you tell us about that debate?

Mojon: It was very important to have that debate. It was a first. You have to understand—now, there are basically two Presidential "elections" in France, because, on the one side, you have five candidates who have been labelled the big candidates, or the major candidates. And you have six other candidates, who have been labelled the minor candidates—they are the outsiders. It's incredible, because you have a huge discrepancy in treatment between the two "elections," so to speak. This debate was very important, because it brought all the candidates together before all the citizens, and broke this separation between two groups of Presidential campaigns. And what everyone noticed was that the "minor" Presidential candidates were indeed much more interesting than the other ones. With some differences, of course.

It was a kind of electric shock. It was very interesting. For Jacques, there was one segment in which he addressed Emmanuel Macron, who was one of these "major" candidates, and Marine Le Pen, another. We made a little video which garnered a great many view-ers. He said, "You guys, you pretend to be this, and you pretend to be that—but the truth is that both of you—you are under the domination of these financial interests."

A second debate was supposed to take place the following Thursday, and the "major" candidates actually conspired to prevent it from happening, because they were so afraid that the "minor" candidates could put them at risk. It was to take place April 20 on France2 public television, but they had to change their plans because they were so afraid of another confrontation with the "minor" candidates. That says a lot about how weak they are—in reality they only represent a caste, they are not free people. And the population knows it, but they are being trapped with the idea that they must not "waste their vote."

Today, a new poll showed two of those major candidates were at an equal 22%, and all the rest were very close to that. There is no one who is clearly ahead. They are freaking out. With only nine days to go before the election, one-third of the electorate has not decided how they'll vote. It's unprecedented. And, you have many people saying they won't vote at all, even though the Presidential election is the main election, the most important election in France.

Jacques Cheminade's Presidential Campaign

by Christine Bierre

PARIS, April 16 (Nouvelle Solidarité)—Jacques Cheminade is running his third presidential campaign in France, much to the dismay of the ruling elites who, under the presidency of François Hollande, did their best to make it very difficult for "minor" candidates to become qualified for the race.

This time around, due undoubtedly to the depth of the crisis in the EU and in France, Jacques Cheminade has been able to address millions on television, and to talk about his program without slanders or innuendos. As of April 10, we are in the last two weeks of the Presidential campaign, leading to the first round vote on April 23, and under the rule of "equality" in media coverage, all candidates will have exactly the same amount of coverage and in equal circumstances.

In this context, Jacques' main campaign themes, "Free France from financial occupation" through Glass-Steagall reform, and by exiting the euro currency, the EU, and NATO, have received massive coverage. The theme of the "financial occupation" of France and the elites "collaborating" with that system, is felt here as a very sharp attack, a shocking attack, because of the Nazi occupation.

Interviewers are intrigued by this idea: "Just who are the financial occupiers?" Cheminade gives examples: In 1979 the French debt was equivalent to 239 billion euros, and it was held essentially by the large French banks; today it is 2.17 trillion euros, and it is

Solidarité & Progrès

Jacques Cheminade on a campaign visit to the Port du Havre.

held by 19 international systemic banks, including major French banks, as well as HSBC, Royal Bank of Scotland, Deutsche Bank, Santander, and UBS, among others. Talking about occupation means also talking about "collaborators" with that system: the large systemic French banks, the 30,000 lobbyists in Brussels, and Mario Draghi's ECB injecting 80 billion euros a month (now 60 billion euros) into the banks.

Also being covered on a daily basis, through several interviews on all national and local media, are Cheminade's long-term proposals to fight for the common aims of mankind as joint projects with other nations:

• For space exploration,

• For exploration and reasonable management of the oceans, whose depths are less known than the surface of the Moon, and are rich with rare metals, and

• For the development of Africa.

Urgently for France, Cheminade's program proposes that once France recovers its economic and financial sovereignty from the EU, and re-establishes its own national bank, he would ossie 100 billion euros in public credit per year, 4.5% of France's GDP, in order to create a million jobs per year in a Rooseveltian manner—going from kindergartens for the very young, to service jobs to aid the seniors, to rebuilding national infrastructure in general and building new infrastructure, and great projects for the future:

• Space,
• Fourth generation nuclear power,
• Fusion power, and
• Robotics.

While some are shocked, and accuse us of wanting to use the printing press to create jobs, Jacques merely refers to the fact that Draghi, a counterfeiter and a

Cheminade Exposes Phony Candidates in April 4 Debate

Cheminade: I want to say something about financial markets. You are a bunch of loudmouths. You try to steal from those who you consider weaker, but the weaker are going to revolt. Mr. Fillon, you talked about debts. They are unjust, illegitimate, and odious debts, as we imposed in the case of Greece! Re-read David Graeber and Ernesto Laclau, and you will see what this debt is. It is debt which has been imposed on the people for the benefit of financial interests. If we do not address this problem, we are not addressing anything!

In 2013, JP Morgan published a paper which I showed the Élysée at the time [he turns to candidate Macron]. The paper said very clearly that the time was over for the constitutions drawn up to protect labor rights in the fight against fascism, that the time was over for all protections of labor, and it was necessary to have authoritarian regimes in the future, maybe on a temporary basis—such as the nationalizations that you propose [said to candidate Hamon] and that they had to be imposed . . . .

former Goldman Sachs boy, is already doing it! Over a year, if one adds 80 billion euros per month of quantitative easing given by Draghi to the European banks, and divides it by 12.5, which is France's part in the European GDP, all this is equivalent to 125 billion euros per year of money printing, which is more than the 100 billion Cheminade is demanding.

Beyond these issues, Jacques has presented innovative ideas for culture, for education, for reintroducing a high level of training in the French high schools, and for modernizing multimodal transport infrastructure and the French strict-sufficiency nuclear deterrent, which is in danger of becoming obsolete.

Cheminade also debated the other ten candidates, live, in a national debate on April 4, organized by the private chain BFM-TV and its affiliates. This was a first ever: the front-runners Marine Le Pen, Emmanuel Macron, François Fillon, Jean-Luc Mélenchon, and Benoit Hamon, agreed to debate the "minor" candidates: Nicolas Dupont Aignan, Jacques Cheminade, Nathalie Arthaud, Philipp Poutou, François Asselineau, and Jean Lassale.

Debate of 11 Candidates

National private channel TF1 had organized a similar debate days before with only the five major candidates, which had provoked a massive outcry, so that these chains felt compelled to keep up the face of democracy. What happened was to be expected: The "minor" candidates bit the "major" ones, causing some visible damage in their poll results. Following this debate, Le Pen and Macron, who, as front runners, were particularly targeted, each lost a point down to 23% and 22% respectively; Fillon went back up to 20%, and Mélenchon gained a point up to 19%. Hamon fell to 7%. The poll results for the "minor" candidates are unknown, because they are all lumped into a single polling figure.

Cheminade was definitely able to call the shots, in particular in the first half of a debate which lasted more than four hours. But many others have helped themselves abundantly, over the years, to Cheminade's proposals, which they add onto their own otherwise-incoherent programs as single issues. Among the candidates, seven want to lift sanctions against Russia, and six are so-called euro-skeptics.

But no one else has the balls to attack the rule of the markets and the financial oligarchy: This was the first polemic Cheminade launched against the two front-runners, Le Pen and Macron. He first turned to Le Pen and brought up the fact that her close financial advisor, Bernard Monot, had proclaimed he is "a man of the markets; our wish is to reassure the financial markets," in an interview after meetings he had with City of London circles who had wanted find out what Le Pen would do if she were elected President. "How will you create the jobs you say you will create, if you accept the rule of the markets which destroy them?" Cheminade asked her, before setting his sights on Macron, saying when you were at the Elysée, you didn't carry

Solidarité & Progrès

Jacques Cheminade in Le Havre, France.

out the banking separation that Hollande had promised, because you did not want to attack the markets. "The common denominator of both: you do not want to attack the markets and you must acknowledge it."

Cheminade moved on to the question of Europe: "The present Europe is destroying itself, and the euro has become a currency of speculation which the ECB's Mario Draghi, a shady banker, manipulates in his own way: passing 80 billion euros per month to the banks in quantitative easing. That is not Europe, it is not the European cathedral wanted by General de Gaulle, Mr. Fillon; it's something else; it is the Europe of 30,000 lobbyists who betray the real Europe, and we must build the real Europe.

And I agree with Asselineau: we must leave the present Europe as it is, i.e. the European Union of the euro, and NATO which is its armed branch—not to jump into the void, but to create a true Europe, another Europe which corresponds to what Charles de Gaulle and the founding fathers had dreamed of: a Europe of nations and projects, of sovereign nation-states—and it's with that Europe that we must move towards great projects. And there, with the BRICS and with China who are proposing a 'win-win' system, this new Europe must ally around a project, another type of economy in the world which will no longer be under the dictates of

the financial markets, but an economy for production, and for the future. You will tell me 'one is never sure of one's partners.' That's true. That's why we must fight with them as one fights with friends and with enemies."

Other key points Cheminade raised are the real fight against terrorism, and the need to eliminate the French currency control in Africa—by means of the African franc (CFA)—and to initiate big projects.

Jacques Cheminade also had a beautiful and unprepared concluding statement. We must, he said, recover the "happy days" of the Libération from the Nazis, but not with the present institutions. We must "free ourselves from the financial and cultural occupation of today."

We must liberate ourselves once again. And for that we must lift the financial occupation that oppresses us, and go for "public credit for the future," banking separation in order to clean up the financial system, and the elimination of despicable debts—for a policy to create real wealth, real growth.

Jacques' Vision for France

"To do that, my fellow Frenchmen must re-establish their self-esteem, rather than being afraid of making mistakes. We must give art and science back to the people, as Leo Lagrange and Jean Vilar had called for.

If that frame of mind is not re-established, people won't fight the way they should. Give everywhere the means to discover, create planetariums, palaces of discovery, and museums of imagination in which the great works of art are made available to all through reproductions, and provoke social ferment like we had in the beginning of the French Revolution, in the villages, among the friendship societies. That is what fraternity means. If you vote for me, you will vote for France seen through the eyes of the Future."

Among the more important statements of Jacques Cheminade on national television in the last two weeks of the campaign, was his 20 minute prime-time interview on TF1, on the evening news, where he was able to address more than five million people. Cheminade was feisty on that interview when the journalists were being nasty.

Following that, Cheminade again toured the country, holding stand-up meetings in the street in Lyon, and in towns of greater Lyon including Villefontaine, and also in Montpellier, in Toulouse—the city which houses all main aerospace industries and research centers. In all these places, some 20 to 40 people gathered around the candidate and asked questions. Some of these standup meetings had been prepared a bit in advance through leafleting and organizing by supporters at public tables for literature distribution. But the participation was good! In the Toulouse area, Cheminade visited an agricultural lab, and a crowd of journalists came to cover him.

Finally, the other very high point of last week was the hour-long prime time morning interview on BFMTV/RMC, with radio star host Jean-Jacques Bourdin, which was excellent from every standpoint. In much of the television coverage, the fact that Jacques is bringing forth Lyndon LaRouche's ideas is brought up, sometimes in a nasty way, sometimes straightforwardly. Most hosts call LaRouche "a conspiracy theorist," but others speak of him without innuendo.

Bourdin presented quotes from an interview Lyndon LaRouche had given to France2 national television in 1995, which was so good that it was never aired. Bourdin presented an extract of LaRouche explaining that in his campaign, Jacques Cheminade was denouncing the Paris elites, who have lost all notion of reality, and went instead to the people in the provinces. After a couple of well-known journalists—Zemmour and Naulleau—tried to corner him into renouncing his friendship with LaRouche by asking "do you admit"

this or that, Cheminade responded, "I fully accept the fact that LaRouche intervened with Foreign Affairs Minister Fred Wills of Guyana at the Colombo conference of the Non-Aligned Movement to call for a new world economic order"; "I fully accept that LaRouche met several times with [then-Indian Prime Minister] Indira Gandhi, and once with [then-Mexican President] José López Portillo, whom he advised to use the 'debt bomb'; I accept that LaRouche met with [then World Jewish Congress president] Nahum Goldmann and with [then-Israeli leader] Abba Eban, and I even accept that once he even supported [then-Israeli Prime Minister] Ariel Sharon who, while not being exactly a dove, was more reasonable than those who succeeded him. …" At this point, the tricked journalist merely said: "Stop!"

Something bigger is happening in France, around Cheminade's campaign. More so than in previous elections, the conditions of a general debate typical of a time of crisis has emerged. In response to Cheminade, a leading group definitely decided that his ideas must be listened to, and proceeded to present many of them during interviews in the form of references to "comparative studies" of all the candidates that had appeared on the Internet. These include Cheminade's answers to questions from specific interest groups. So, over all, if the French people want to know who he is and what he represents, they have many ways to do so, including our own Internet.

The last thing to report is that to this day, one week before the election, the outcome is still not determined. The two front runners: Le Pen and this creature of the banks and the media called Macron, have been losing points (the first is at 23%, the second 22%). In the meantime, Fillon got back up to 20%, and Jean-Luc Mélenchon, who is a French version of the German [leftist] Die Linke, moved up to 19%. This old Mitterrand hand has transformed himself successfully into a mixture of an anti-EU Tsipras and Hugo Chavez, and has taken themes from us like space exploration and banking separation, which, however, he combines with the kiss of death: a call to end de Gaulle's Fifth Republic, and to instead usher in a new parliamentary Third Republic (which they call Sixth), and having France abandon nuclear power in favor of offshore windmills. Whatever the results, however, as Cheminade has stated many times on French television and media recently, there will be no majority in France, so the fight will continue.

Jacques Cheminade Meets Lebanese President, Works To Bring Peace Throughout the Middle East

by Christine Bierre

April 9 (EIRNS)—On April 7, just hours after President Trump had been misled into ordering an attack on a Syrian airbase at al-Shairat, French Presidential candidate Jacques Cheminade met Lebanese President Michel Aoun at the Lebanese Baabda presidential palace, to talk about "peace through development" for the entire region. Christine Bierre, in charge of this region for Cheminade's movement, also attended the meeting.

After that 30-minute meeting, Cheminade made the following remarks to the press gathered at the presidential palace.

"I have come to Lebanon in the spirit of a Free Lebanon, over and above all political factions, as one should always approach such things

Solidarité & Progrès

President of Lebanon Michel Aoun (right) greets Jacques Cheminade in Lebanon, April 7, 2017.

in France, and to show the role Lebanon can play in the Middle East and in world affairs. For a long time now, in particular since February 1989, General Aoun has been very important in this respect, because he has always shown great political courage and great independent-mindedness, nurtured by his political courage.

"Today, I have come here to say that France must do everything to support the cause of Lebanon, and in particular to make sure that Europe and France contribute much more aid to the political and economic refugees fleeing to Lebanon, as well as to those in Lebanon who receive the refugees and who sometimes live less well than they [the refugees] do. France must do all in her power to deal with that question. We know that there are between 2 and 2.5 million refugees in

Lebanon, which has a population of 4.5 million inhabitants. We must absolutely do something to help Lebanon.

"The way to help in a decisive manner is to allow the refugees to return to their countries, in particular to Syria, and to help by creating conditions of peace in Syria, through economic development and reconstruction. We did this in France after World War II, with public credit and a commitment to the future. Today we need credit for the development of Syria, so that the Syrians can go back to their country and live there. With time—and that time must be as short as possible—that is the only way to establish peace, through mutual development in the Near and Middle East.

"What happened today at dawn—the missiles fired from an American vessel at an important Syrian base—is something that will no doubt worsen what is happening here. It was carried out before an international investigation into what had really happened in Syria could occur, and it was a decision by President Trump, to go far beyond what Obama did in 2013, when Obama stopped before launching missiles.

"In my opinion, there has been, in a totally premature manner, a violation of the sovereignty of one nation by another one. I think this is very serious. It does not help peace in the Near and Middle East in any way—and we must very quickly, without losing time in useless debates, say that this intervention in the internal affairs of a state must stop, and we must instead create the conditions for peace through mutual development in the future. From that standpoint, Lebanon and the Lebanon of General Aoun must play an absolutely fundamental role that France must recognize."

In further remarks during that day, Jacques Cheminade referred to the hypocrisy and cynicism of those in France and the Western nations who are calling for a coalition against Assad. "I am not for a coalition against Bashar al-Assad," he told the correspondent of the French national all-business BFM TV, "but in favor of stabilizing the situation in Lebanon. Some continuously preach morality; the reality is that those doing the moralizing are the ones who organized the military intervention in Libya with the consequences we know, and who allow Yemen to be bombed by Saudi Arabia. They even give the Saudis more intelligence to be able to better bomb Yemen, and after that, they give lessons on morality to the entire world. I find that to be of the utmost hypocrisy and cynicism."

Cheminade told Radio France Internationale (RFI), "Politics is not to be nice to someone's face, and cynical behind his back. Politics is what General de Gaulle did, which is to try by all means to reach détente, entente, and cooperation" among all nations.

Finally, Cheminade expressed his concern with the serious problems Lebanon is facing today due to the war against Syria. To a question by a Lebanese journalist following his meeting at Baabda, Cheminade said that he talked with President Aoun "about pressing France and Europe for more help to urgently improve the sanitation systems currently in a catastrophic state due to the occupation of a country of only 4.5 million inhabitants by too many refugees." President Aoun had said Europe had begun to help, but Cheminade said that aid must go much further, indicating that France's world-class water companies should be brought in to contribute to solve those problems.

An article in the April 8 issue of the main French-language Lebanese daily *l'Orient le Jour* also reported that Cheminade was in Lebanon to "to support a Free Lebanon ... beyond its political divisions," to pay homage to Aoun's "political courage" and "independent mindedness," and to call for more aid to Lebanon to solve its domestic difficulties due to the refugee crisis.

"Lebanon could become a powder keg," he warned, in his interview to BFM TV, and for that reason "the refugees must be able to go back to Syria and the conditions must be created for them to do so, rather than creating dissensions and tensions through interventions like that of Trump."

Lebanon is exemplary, he said, "because there have been all these family quarrels, with killings and murders; it's almost Shakespearean, with the Hariris, the Geageas, the Frangiehs, and the Gemayels as examples. But Aoun came and succeeded in creating unity among those people who thought about the future of the country. It is that attitude that we must have throughout the whole region."

Cheminade concluded his trip to Lebanon in discussion with a few Frenchmen—potential voters—who attended a meeting that the candidate organized that evening.

Every Day Counts In Today's Showdown To Save Civilization

That's why you need EIR's **Daily Alert Service**, a strategic overview compiled with the input of Lyndon LaRouche, and delivered to your email 5 days a week.

The election of Donald Trump to the Presidency of the Untied States has launched a new global era whose character has yet to be determined. The Obama-Clinton drive toward confrontation with Russia has been disrupted--but what will come next?

Over the next weeks and months there will be a pitched battle to determine the course of the Trump Administration. Will it pursue policies of cooperation with Russia and China in the New Silk Road, as the President-Elect has given some signs of? Will it follow through against Wall Street with Glass-Steagall?

The opposition to these policies will be fierce. If there is to be a positive outcome to this battle, an informed citizenry must do its part--intervening, educating, inspiring. That's why you need the EIR Daily Alert more than ever.

TUESDAY, NOVEMBER 22, 2016

Volume 3, Number 65

EIR Daily Alert Service

P.O. Box 17390, Washington, DC 20041-0390

- Only Global Solutions, Based on New Principles, Can Work
- Tulsi Gabbard Meets with Donald Trump Regarding Syria
- Robert Kagan Throws in the Towel, Complains U.S. Is Becoming 'Solipsistic'
- War Party Moving To Preempt Trump-Putin Reset
- Syrian Army Makes More Progress in Aleppo
- Duterte Gives OK to Nuclear Power for Philippines
- Europe Will Suffer from Maintaining Russia Sanctions
- Former Chilean Diplomat Confirmed, 'We Will Joyfully Welcome Xi Jinping'
- Duterte and Putin Establish Philippines-Russia Cooperation
- François Fillon, Pro-Russian Thatcherite, Wins First Round of French Right-Wing Presidential Primary

EDITORIAL

Only Global Solutions, Based on New Principles, Can Work

III. First-Hand Report from Syria

STATE SEN. RICHARD BLACK

'No Chance That Was a Poison Gas Attack by the Syrian Government'

The following LaRouche PAC interview with Virginia State Senator Richard Black took place on April 10.

Matthew Ogden: We are joined today by State Senator Richard Black, who is from the 13th District of Virginia. He is also a combat veteran, served with the U.S. Marine Corps in Viet Nam, from 1963 to 1970, and then served in the Army as Judge Advocate General from 1976 to 1994. We are very happy to have you join us here today, Senator.

Sen. Richard Black: I'm very pleased to be with you today.

Ogden: Now I should tell our viewers that a little over one year ago, you personally visited Syria in the spring of 2016. While you were in Syria, you had the opportunity to meet with the leading members of the Syrian military; you toured the country, you visited the liberated city of Palmyra, the ancient city which was liberated from ISIS forces by the Syrian government, and you also ultimately had the chance to meet directly with President Bashar al Assad, along with his wife, the first lady of Syria. You had the interest to visit Syria, to visit the country, to be on the ground, to witness first-hand what the reality of the situation was there.

Now, in the days following the missile strike last week that was ordered by President Trump on the Syrian airbase in response to the alleged chemical warfare attack on civilians by the Syrian government, you have been very vocal in your opposition to those attacks and your warnings about what the implications of further escalation could mean.

I want to display on the screen right now a tweet that you sent out immediately following those attacks, which has been retweeted over 3,000 times. That tweet reads as follows:

"If we go into Syria, we are entering World War three based upon information provided by terrorists. If we topple Assad, we help ISIS." And you directed that to President Donald Trump.

So, to begin our discussion here today, I would just like to invite you to elaborate on the point you made in that tweet.

Black: Just today, word has come out in the press that Russia and Iran made a very clear statement that they will no longer simply stand aside when we decide that we are going to go in, and we are going to attack. They are going to respond. We are moving quite rapidly toward a potential showdown between the United States and Russia. There are some people I believe who are looking for that to happen, and are trying to make it occur. And of course, it would be a monumental disaster. The people who are willing to risk that are basing it on the assumption that we can beat Russia militarily, and I think what they better remember is that both sides have roughly 1,500 fully operational, ready to go thermonuclear missiles, enough to essentially obliterate both Russia and the United States; so we are in a time of enormous recklessness. You never would have seen this during the Cold War, when Americans down to the level of children, recognized the tremendous danger that the world faced from a thermonuclear war. We need to wake up very quickly.

Ogden: LaRouche PAC recently posted a statement on our website which contains a warning from Mr. LaRouche personally about who it is that is attempting to draw the United States back into this confrontation with Russia. It reads:

"Lyndon LaRouche warned today that there is a British run coup d'état in process against the Trump administration in the United States, which threatens to parlay the stupid and dangerous April 6th airstrike against Syria into a full-fledged thermonuclear confrontation with Russia and China... It's the British bastards who duped Donald Trump into attacking Syria with their lies and false intelligence. We have to destroy this operation and all the British interests in the U.S.," Mr. LaRouche stated. "We have to rally the U.S. to get back on the trajectory Trump had begun to chart for the country, of cooperation with Russia and China around American System economic policies, including FDR's 1933 Glass Steagall." And then the call to action is the following: "Trump and Putin should immediately hold a summit meeting to address the crisis, and thereby short circuit the whole British operation."

What's your response to that, Senator?

Black: I agree with it. I noticed that the British Foreign Minister has called on us to show a united front with respect to Russia. I don't want a united front; I want the United States to talk with Russia. I don't want some globalist cabal to do this. I think President Putin is a man who is very rational; he is not given to emotional outbursts or anything of that sort. He is very methodical, and I think Donald Trump probably needs to sit down with him, not in some sort of contentious thing, but simply look at things in an analytical fashion. *We do not need the British trying to push us into additional confrontation with Russia.* We are already far too far down that line where we are engaging in unnecessary confrontational behavior toward Russia, with absolutely no rational justification.

Let me just mention, just for your listeners to know: I am not a professional anti-war activist; I was wounded fighting in Viet Nam; my radio men were killed right

Flickr/Frank Balsinger

Al Nusra Front executions. Image, as released by Al Nusra Front, posted at Threat Matrix.

beside me fighting with the First Marine Regiment. I was also a pilot, and I flew 269 combat missions, came back with bullet holes in the plane on four of those missions. I've probably seen as much combat and as fierce combat as anybody in Congress and most of the people in the Administration. So I come at it from a very rational and very logical standpoint, and I see the United States on an utterly suicidal path right now. My objective is to save the lives of not only Americans, but also of people in the Mideast. We are wiping the Christian communities out— communities that have been there for 2,000 years—and I don't want to see Christians wiped out; I don't want to see Muslims wiped out. I want to see a return to peace.

What Motive?

And so as I looked at this, you know, I was the top prosecutor in the Pentagon; I was the chief of the Criminal Law Division, and I got there through a career of prosecutions; and I'll tell you that one of the things that a prosecutor does is he looks at a motive. If you're looking at someone's wife who has been killed, you ask, "did he just take out an insurance policy on her life?" What is the reason? There is something that always prompts these types of things. So, when I look at it, I look at it from the standpoint of a prosecutor. What would have been a possible motive for President Assad to launch a poison-gas attack on the terrorist positions?

Well, first of all, he didn't launch them on the terrorist positions. The bombs that were dropped were targeted on a warehouse that was owned by the terrorists, and, assuming that the truth is that there were people killed in a gas attack—and I'm inclined to believe that, that there was gas released—the question is, what would be the reason for President Assad to snatch defeat from the jaws of victory? He is winning the war on virtually every front. Now, if he were to use poison-gas—and we know that most of it was evacuated from the country—but if he were to use it, why would he use it on a handful of civilians walking out in the street? Why would he not use it against enemy armored formations, or against heavily entrenched terrorists? Those are the people that his troops are fighting against daily and taking casualties daily—why would he instead turn around and say, "Oh, we don't have the weapons to use against the enemy troops; we'll kill some women and kids." This is so childishly irrational that you would think that any responsible person would understand it.

Another thing we know is that, under the protocols established between Syria, Russia and the United States, there is an agreement that Syria will advise the United States of any flights, so there is an arrangement that exists to prevent inadvertent problems. The Syrians notified the United States before they made their flight. Look: If you're going to commit a war crime, you're certainly not going to notify the other side and say, hey, by the way, we're about to launch this attack. This was a standard bombing attack on a terrorist warehouse. What makes us think that the gas was not released from chemical weapons that were stored in the warehouse that Syria was bombing? Why did we suddenly jump to the conclusion that it was the bombs that released gas rather than the warehouse that was being bombed?

Now, some people say, "well we know it's the Syrians who have gas." Well, first of all, we don't know for a fact that Syrians have gas any longer. What we do know for a fact is that CNN reported on September 13, 2016, which is just five months ago, that the U.S. had launched a major bombing attack on an ISIS poison gas factory in Mosul. This was such a large attack that we used B-52 bombers in doing it. We know without question, that the terrorists have poison gas. They have been using it throughout the war; they used it in a false flag attack on Damascus back in 2013, the one people keep referring to as the red line [violation], but in fact the [violation was done by] the terrorists working together with Turkish intelligence. So we know. I mean, just five months ago the U.S. bombed an ISIS poison gas factory in Mosul; and so how is it that we make our conclusion that this was an attack of gas from the Syrians? It just does not make any sense.

Also, something that as a prosecutor you look at is, "what's the source of the evidence?" "What is the credibility of witnesses?" *All of the witnesses are terrorists that are associated with ISIS and Al Qaeda. There are no neutral people on the ground there.* There are no Syrian government troops who are present where this bombing took place. Part of the evidence came from a group called the White Helmets. The White Helmets are an element of Al-Qaeda. And Americans need to remember: It was Al-Qaeda that killed 3,000 Americans on 9/11. How credible are witnesses who were involved in attacks that brought down the Twin Towers and part of the Pentagon on 9/11? You look at the people who are celebrating the [U.S. strike]: Nancy Pelosi, Hillary Clinton, the Saudi Arabians, John McCain—people who have been integrally involved in a whole series of wars that have inflamed the Mideast and have caused death and destruction of Sunnis, of Shi'ites, of Christians, people of a number of nations. These are the people who are cheering on the attack. And I think it's very unfortunate. I oppose these attacks unequivocally. *I think there is no chance whatsoever that there was a poison gas attack launched by the Syrian government.*

The Battle Within the Trump Administration

Ogden: Now, during the campaign and even in his opening days as President of the United States, Donald Trump was clear, questioning why should we trust an intelligence community that got it so wrong with weapons of mass destruction in Iraq? What credibility do they have?

But now President Trump has ordered a missile strike against President Bashar al-Assad's forces. We saw a complete pivot, a 180 degree turnaround. The question is what happened? What are your insights into what could possibly have happened behind the scenes to induce such a radical change in policy from the Trump Administration.

Black: I think there is a struggle going on within the Trump Administration. Probably the most valuable member of the Administration who was ousted was Michael Flynn. Michael Flynn was a very well informed, very intelligent individual. He was ousted for virtually no reason whatsoever; it was just all of these fallacious claims that were made, and they for whatever reason let him go. That was disastrous to Trump when it came to foreign affairs, because Michael Flynn understood—this would not have happened with him. I worry about the rapid turnover taking place in the Trump Administration. We've never seen any administration in my lifetime that has had this constant churning of people. K.T. McFarland has just been moved out of the White House. So I think we have this struggle going on between those who stand for peace and those who benefit from war.

There are certain things that earn enormous sums of money, and they are, essentially, war, oil and drugs. And the amount of money that flows from those things is just phenomenal. It is beyond the ability of most people to comprehend, but you're talking about tens, hundreds of billions of dollars that are made from wars, from the manipulation of the oil markets, and from the drug transactions flowing around the world. And so you have this group of people who are influenced by those people with the vast sums of money and influence.

On the other hand, on the side of peace, all you have is just ordinary citizens with social media and what little they can muster, and we use logic whereas they use the tools that Josef Goebbels used with the Nazis, the mass media, the things of that sort. They were saying that one of things that influenced President Trump was looking at an image of a small girl who had supposedly been killed by gas. Now that certainly is a sad thing; but I will tell you, I have seen, I have personally watched videos of at least a thousand Syrians beheaded, crucified, cannibalized, burned alive, all of these things. There are plenty of images. If you want images, I could show you an image, I don't care how hardened you are, it would certainly evoke an emotional response.

Muslim Brotherhood, Ambassador Ford

We have to get away from relying on propaganda and emotionalism to make foreign policy. We've got to come up with a rational foreign policy based on known facts, and we need to keep in mind also, there is the Deep State. During the years of Obama and Clinton, there have been people put in place within the Federal bureaucracy, and those people are ideologically committed. Many people were placed in intelligence positions and foreign policy positions who are associated with the Muslim Brotherhood. And so the Muslim Brotherhood has its impact on our foreign policy. This is a very, very bad thing. Interestingly, the President of Egypt, who is one of the finest leaders in the world, in my personal opinion, had a wonderful visit with Donald Trump a week ago, and it was very warm; it was a tremendous visit. He went back to Egypt. When Syria was bombed, President Abdel Fattah El-Sisi put out a statement condemning the bombing. This shows he is a man who is driven by logic, by rational thought, and not by simple emotionalism or knee-jerk reactions. We have got to get a firm hand on foreign policy, or we are going to stumble our way into a nuclear war.

Ogden: The warning is coming from various quarters that this so-called deep state apparatus that you just raised, stay-behinds from the Obama and other administrations, that this apparatus is now in the process of waging a slow motion soft coup against the Trump Administration, and that this is threatening to split the Administration apart and severely weaken it, if not bring it down. Is that something you see as a danger here? And I should say you were a supporter of President Trump during the campaign, perhaps because of his opposition to these regime-change wars, but so many of his supporters are very horrified at what they now see coming out of this Administration in terms of this radical change in military policy toward Syria.

Black: I was perhaps as prominent as anyone in the state of Virginia in my support for Donald Trump. I gave the major speech for him in Richmond, right after his nomination. I gave the major speech for him in Leesburg, Virginia when he made his final swing the night before Election Day. I've been a strong supporter of his. But a portion of that was that I believed that he was going to draw back from the policy of regime change and incessant war that's bankrupted this country. We're $20 trillion in debt. If we were a company, someone would call the debt and petition the bankruptcy court, and we'd be thrown into bankruptcy tomorrow. So we don't have the money to afford to be fighting, sending our military as mercenaries for Saudi Arabia and Qatar and Turkey and all of these other filthy regimes that are truly as brutal and barbaric as any on the face of the earth.

Something interesting: Ambassador Robert Ford was involved; he was actually instrumental in creating the revolution against the Syrian government. When there were demonstrations, he and the French ambassador broke diplomatic protocols. They went to one of the major cities where there was a demonstration under way. They circumvented the government forces that had blocked off the city, and they met with the demonstrators, and they pledged firm American support for the demonstrators, and this as much as anything turned peaceful demonstrations into an armed revolution.

Ambassador Ford was quoted in the newspaper just today, saying—now that we know that the terrorists have gotten away with another false flag attack, just as they did in 2013—he's predicting many more [attacks "by Assad"]... How does he know this? He knows this because he knows that once Al-Qaeda and ISIS get away with a false flag attack, and they know that the media will quickly pick it up, they're bound to do it again. And, unfortunately, I think some of these attacks are being planned with the help of elements within the covert intel-

Flickr/U.S. Department of State

U.S. Ambassador to Syria Robert Ford talks with Syrian refugees at Islahiye Refugee Camp in Turkey, January 24, 2013.

ligence communities of several countries, some of them Western countries. And I think Ambassador Ford understands our reaction to this; the rash reaction that we had was simply an invitation for the terrorists to stage another similar attack and to draw us into the war more deeply than we are now.

Stop Arming the Terrorists

Ogden: My final question for you calls for one more insight that I think you are uniquely positioned to give. What is the actual solution to the crisis in Syria? If you were to have the opportunity to sit down with President Trump right now and say, "What you did was a disaster. Here is the only way it can be cleaned up and fixed, and here is how we can actually bring peace to Syria and to that entire region of the Middle East and North Africa"—What would you say?

Black: The first thing is to recognize who the parties to the conflict are. There are essentially two parties. One is the Syrian government with its allies. The other is al-Qaeda with its allies. There are the terrorists and there is the legitimate, duly elected, popularly elected government of Syria. That is, the first thing is to understand who the enemy is. The enemy is not the President who has been elected by some eighty percent of the Syrian people. It is the terrorists. We need to recognize that in the six years we have been trying to overthrow their government, there has not been a single coup attempt against President Assad. Even though he is not heavily defended. He has rather light security. We need to recognize the people of Syria are totally loyal to him. There are terrorists out there that are on the other side, but probably eighty percent of Syria are under government control and are delighted to be there; and of the ones

under terrorist control, probably two thirds of them wish they could be under government control. So we need to understand who is the enemy, who is the legitimate government of Syria. That is number one.

Now, the United States, beginning around 2011, 2012, set up terrorist training camps in Jordan, Turkey, Qatar and Saudi Arabia. We train terrorists from many different Islamic states; we pay them; we give them arms training, and then we send them to units, and essentially they go onto an open market. I recall reading a comment from an ISIS leader and he said, "Where do you think we get our people? They come from the training camps the Americans set up"! We are training the troops that are fighting against Syria and fighting against the world. We need to stop arming the terrorists. I have discovered that all of the Toyota vehicles that are used over there—they mount canon on them and it's a rather inexpensive military vehicle—they're made in San Antonio, Texas. They're not made in Japan. We ship them over. There is one of the models that comes with a very heavy radiator suspension and so forth, and then they go to Croatia where they have canon mounted on them, and then back through Turkey, and then they're fed out to all the terrorist organizations. We need to stop sending the trucks.

We also have been providing TOW anti-tank missiles. When Russia went in and sent their expeditionary forces there, it turned the war dramatically. The war would have probably been over in a year and a half. The United States rushed vast supplies of TOW anti-tank missiles and blunted the advance of Syrian military forces. If we hadn't sent those TOW anti-tank missiles, the war would be over, the refugees would be flooding back to Syria, people would be rebuilding, the economy would be thriving. So we need to stop that.

Another thing we need to do. We have placed absolutely inhuman sanctions on Syria. Not only are they sanctions against what you can send, but we shut down the financial transaction system, so they can't move money around, and as a consequence the Syrian people are being deprived of food. It costs half a week's wages to buy one pound of potatoes for a family. So obviously, we're causing widespread hunger, which is illegal under the Law of Land Warfare. Also, we are blocking medications from getting in. Cancer medications are blocked. Prosthetic devices are being blocked. Again, a clear violation of international law, but we do it because the Deep State is determined that they are going to bring down this small nation of twenty-three million people.

The Syrians have fought one of the most heroic wars in the history of mankind. Twenty-three million people—and they have fought against the United States, Britain, France, NATO, the Gulf States, Turkey, Saudi Arabia, Qatar, Kuwait. A huge array of the wealthiest countries on Earth, and they have withstood them for six years. They did not do that without having confidence in their government and in their army, and unity among the people. So we need to stop arming the terrorists. As you know, Representative Tulsi Gabbard, liberal Democrat from Hawaii, and Senator Rand Paul, conservative Republican from Kentucky, have each introduced a bill called the "Stop Arming Terrorists Act." Can you imagine that we have to introduce legislation to stop our government from arming the people who brought down the Twin Towers on 9/11?

It is stunning. It is an act of treason of breathtaking magnitude, and we need to stop it.

We've Got to Win this Battle

Ogden: One year ago, LaRouche PAC produced a documentary called "Project Phoenix: the Program for the Reconstruction of Syria," which lays out the vision for the economic development of Syria as a hub for economic activity for the entire region and as a bridge between cultures. One of the major aspects of this was that Syria is uniquely situated to join the New Silk Road economic development project which has been initiated by China and many other nations. This is something Syria should have access to.

Black: Yes, there is plenty of wealth to be made. If the global oligarchs want to become wealthy, they can back something like the Silk Road, but it won't be just to the oligarchs; it will be to the common people, whether they be in the Middle East, Africa, the United States, or South America—but today one of our major exports is war. I look at the countries that make and create wars, and I'm sorry to say that ours is one of the principal ones. Probably after us, the one that threatens the greatest amount of warfare is our dear ally the Turks, who are trying to reconstruct the Ottoman Empire and who have flooded arms and vicious jihadists across their border into Syria. I really hope and I pray that we will have a change in the course that we have taken, because it leads ultimately to the third world war. I do not want my children dying in a war for the global oligarchs who will not send their children, but they will send our children off to die, to lose their arms, their legs, their sight. I'm finished with it. I'm not going to participate in that again.

I know a lot of people are shy about making a call to a Congressman's office, but... we need to rise up. Do it for your children. Do it for your grandchildren. Do it for

Office of Representative Gabbard

Rep. Tulsi Gabbard at the ceremony of her promotion to Major on October 12, 2015.

your husband, your wife. We do not need to have the nation mobilized for the third world war. When you call your representative you'll get the congressional switchboard, and you just say, "please give me Senator Tim Kaine," or "give me Congressman Comstock's office," they will send you to that office. You will get one of the assistants in the office, and they're not going to argue or fight with you. Simply say, "I want to register my strong opposition to the U.S. attack on Syria," and they will say thank you very much, they will put an x on the box, and then that will go to the Congressman, and the Congressman will say, "Wow, there are a lot of people against this," and it will have an effect.

Ogden: Do you have any concluding words for us?

Black: I applaud you for the work you are doing on the Silk Road. I think it's a very good initiative—and thank you so much for mobilizing people. It is much easier to stop a war than it is to go through a war. I go down to Bethesda, Walter Reed Hospital, and it just breaks my heart. I walk past so many people: young, vibrant, men and women who are being wheeled around, and they've lost their legs, they've lost their arms, they've lost their eyesight—and for what? And I bless them, I love them all, I respect them. They followed their nation's call, but when the wrong people are calling and they are calling for the wrong reasons, we've got to stop them.

So, thank you so much for letting me be on, today. And let's all fight. We've got to win this battle. This is essential.

IV. LaRouche in 2002 on Science and Empire

Does Technology Steal Jobs?

The Luddites and Malthusians of times past have died, but their pernicious ideology lives on. An analysis by Lyndon H. LaRouche, Jr.

May 21, 2002

Technology does not "steal jobs." Yet, still today, one sometimes hears the defense of that myth from surprising sources. Therefore, I supply a fresh, up-to-date overview of the essential history of that delusion. This may also clarify some other important issues posed by the onrushing collapse of the present world monetary-financial system.

The celebrated Cambridge University trio of students, Babbage, Herschel,[1] and Peacock, wrote a paper of extraordinary importance for the political history of modern science. This paper, which is sometimes known by the short title of "D-ism and Dot-age," effectively ridiculed the backwardness of science in early Nineteenth-Century Benthamite England. This inferiority of England's science to that of continental Europe and also the U.S.A. during those decades, continued to be a leading concern of the collaborators Herschel and Babbage. It was this shared concern, which among its other outcomes, led Babbage to develop the conceptual design of the principles of the operator-programmable, mid-Twentieth-Century electronic digital computer.

It was partly in reaction to the impact of the argument by Herschel and Babbage on Britain's economic backwardness, that mid-Nineteenth-Century Britain put aside the anti-science cult called "Luddism." This shift, in favor of at least a degree of technological progress, was expressed by the establishment of the delphic dogma of the British Association for the Advancement of Science (BAAS) and the echoed launching of the American Association for the Advancement of Science (AAAS).[2]

It was against that strategic background, including the U.S. defeat of the Anglo-French-sponsored Confederacy, that the British monarchy began mobilizing technologically for what became both new strategic operations against the U.S.A., and the future two World Wars on the continent of Europe. The strategic ironies of the present-day U.S. lunge toward global perpetual war, are, as I shall show, in significant part, a reflection of same issues posed by the "geopolitical" heritage of that part of the history of England which led into the establishment of the BAAS.

Nonetheless, the threatened resurgence of something like "Luddism" continued to suppurate in Britain.

It was during the 1790s, during the time under chief ideologue Jeremy Bentham, when Britain was a scientific backwater of European civilization, that the British monarchy produced the English translation of a book, on the subject of population control, by the Venetian-school Italian, Giammaria Ortes. The doctrine which the British East India Company's Reverend Malthus copied from that book, became known, therefore, as the "Malthusian" dogma of Prime Minister William Pitt the Younger. This, and the cult of Darwinism derived from it, became part of the dogma of the British East India Company's Haileybury School's economists, Adam Smith, Malthus, Ricardo, et al.

For a time, to aid in enforcing that Malthusian backwardness, the Benthamites deployed the terrorist Luddite "machine breakers." Ever since, the sophistry has spread among susceptible circles of trade-unionists and

---

1. The son of England's leading scientist, the astronomer William Herschel, and, later, a leading astronomer in his own right.

2. It is to be noted, as the influence of Kelvin and written declarations of J. Clerk Maxwell, and London's asset Hermann Helmholtz attest, that BAAS and related policy "borrowed" much of the fruits of Nineteenth-Century German science, but never accepted the core of the method which produced those benefits.

An anti-logging demonstration by the eco-terrorist group Earth First!, in Eureka, California, during the 1990s; and the group's "how-to" manual for destroying industrial machinery.

socialists, that "technology steals jobs." The Luddites of times past died, but the myth lived on. The impact of that continuing myth, later surfaced under different rubrics, including the neo-feudalist "guild socialism" of Oxford's John Ruskin, and of such avowed British fascists from among the George Bernard Shaw and H.G. Wells circles, as the utopian so-called "Distributists" G.K. Chesterton and Hilaire Belloc.

Unfortunately, many economists, and others who remain more or less illiterates respecting the rudiments of the science of physical economy, have been duped into adopting some of the residue of the Luddite myth, still today. As I summarize the relevant point here, the proof of the absurdity of that myth, is elementary, but there are also some other important points to be considered as indispensable, for studying that topic in a present-day context.

The myth resurfaced among the circles of H.G. Wells and Bertrand Russell during the decades preceding World War II. The form of the Malthusian myth associated with the utopians Wells and Russell, gained increasing hegemony in intellectually polluted science centers of the world during the post-1945 decades, leading to the virtual hegemony of Malthusian cults, not only among the generation entering universities from the mid-1960s, onward, but as leading strategic policies of the U.S. government, under the Kissinger-managed Nixon Administration, and the Wellsian-uto-pian Zbigniew Brzezinski's control over the Carter candidacy and Administration.[3]

1. What Is True About Economies?

Among reasonable people, the definition of truth is the modern Socratic notion, that *truth is that which can be demonstrated to be universally true, at least in such a fair approximation as Kepler's original (1609) account of his discovery of a universal physical principle of gravitation.* Therefore, all attempt to prove the generality of an alleged principle, such as the assertion that "technology steals jobs," is already shown to be false, merely by examining the fallacy of composition inhering axiomatically in the method employed to build an apparent statistical case for the pro-Malthusian and kindred "ecological" arguments still today.

This definition of all truthful notions of universal principle, is a crucial consideration emphasized in Bernhard Riemann's 1854 habilitation dissertation, in

---

3. Henry Kissinger's "National Security Study Memorandum 200: Implications of Worldwide Population Growth for U.S. Security and Overseas Interests," Dec. 10, 1974 (later declassified), branded the growth of populations in selected Third World countries as a threat to U.S. national security. See excerpts in **EIR**, June 9, 1995. See also the State Department's **Global 2000 Report to the President,** 1980 (excerpts in **EIR**, March 10, 1981).

John Herschel (left) and Charles Babbage, who ridiculed the backwardness of science in early-Nineteenth-Century England.

which he included two warnings relevant to the matter under discussion here. First, in his concluding point, he states that nothing can be proven true by mathematics at the blackboard; truth in mathematics is a question of physics, not mathematics.[4] In the course of that same dissertation, he emphasized, second, that physical proof of a universal principle, requires the evidence of a unique class of experiments.

Typical of the continued development of that Keplerian, Riemannian, etc. generality of the experimental class of universal physical principles, is Vladimir Vernadsky's experimental partition of the physical universe among three phase-spaces: the abiotic; the anti-entropic domain of living processes and their fossil effects (the Biosphere); and the anti-entropic domain of human cognitive processes and the physical effects (e.g., "fossils") uniquely products of such activity (the Noösphere). Real economies are to be subsumed under the definition of the Noösphere.[5]

Implicitly, as my own work has emphasized this point, Vernadsky's definition of the Noösphere goes to a point just short of what I have shown, that economic processes could never be understood, until it is recognized that the notion of universal physical principles must be extended to include valid universal conceptions of Classical artistic composition. This latter set of artistic principles includes the principles of *bel canto*-based, well-tempered counterpoint of J.S. Bach, and such as those notions of the respectively tragic and sublime, as efficiently universal physical principles of Classical drama and poetry.

Any adducible principle, including principles of Classical artistic composition, which can be demonstrated to have a uniquely defined efficient effect on society's increased physical power over the Noösphere, is also a universal physical principle of the Noösphere, that by virtue of its physical effects. The cognitive principle of truthful, anti-symbolic ambiguity, called *irony*, the same principle of *cognitive intention* expressed in Kepler's discovery of a principle of universal gravitation, is what distinguishes Classical artistic composition from all other, and defines the pivotal physical feature of the quality of such art as expressing physical principles of the Noösphere.[6]

The minimal experimental base for general statements respecting economic processes, is the study of the integral entirety of a national economy from the standpoint of physical economy, rather than that of financial accounting methods. However, that is not sufficient. Even studies premised on the notions of physical economy, would be more or less fatally flawed, if the interacting physical economies of the world at large, were not taken adequately into account in composing the proposition applied to study of any particular national economy. Errors of both types fall under the classification of "fallacies of composition" of the evidence considered. That much said, the general outline of the required procedure, is as follows.

Any competent definition of the universal principles of a physical economy, arises out of an experimentally oriented reflection on the notion of measuring changes in *the potential relative population-density* of an economy which is considered as approximately a functionally unified whole.[7] This must be measured in terms of a functionally definable net increase in physical output per capita and per square kilometer of surface-area. This must be measured relative to a correlated improvement in the demographic characteristics internal to the

---

4. This was also the essential argument of Kepler, in his 1609 report of the original discovery of a universal physical principle of gravitation.
5. Cf. Lyndon H. LaRouche, Jr. **The Economics of the Noösphere** (Washington, D.C.: EIR News Service, 2001).

6. Ibid.
7. Lyndon H. LaRouche, Jr. **Now, Are You Ready to Learn Economics?** (Washington, D.C.: EIR News Service, 2000).

population, the latter considered as a whole. In such measurements, it is required that there be no lowering of demographic characteristics in any significant portion of that population as a whole.

The emphasis of the measurement must be on the rate of change of that potential relative population-density, rather than a comparison of fixed rates. This must be defined within the framework of a long-range cycle, and must take into account the functionally defined shifts in relations between the society and the Biosphere. The requirement is, for a net increase in the rate of increase of potential relative population-density, taking into account the interdependency of society and Biosphere.

This requirement, for measuring performance by a function of change, rather than relative values of what are apparently current ratios, is demonstrated by reexamining the momentary situation expressed in short-term estimates, from the standpoint of medium- to long-range cycles, in which the impact of the past upon the present is expressed, and also of the past and present, combined, upon the future. The ability of the present and future combined, to change the quality of outcome of what had been mistakenly thought to have been buried with the past, is the ironical fact which rips apart all pedantic studies of history, economy included, and exposes the notion of simple sense-certainty of the here and now, as a bad joke.

The issue of method posed by such longer-range studies, is a reflection of the same principled problem which Kepler faced in adducing a universal function underlying the determination of short-term orbital motion. The partial and local must be defined from the starting-point of reference to their place within the determining characteristics of the process as a whole.

This quality of potential expressed in long-range economic cycles, is specific to humanity; it is willful in its human-specific, functionally *anti-entropic* characteristics; and, it does not exist among any lower living species. *Within the bounds of a Riemannian mathematical physics, this anti-entropic quality is typified by the quality of change of a given manifold, by the addition of an applied original discovery of an experimentally valid universal physical principle.*[8]

That latter consideration poses the notion of the nature of the function expressed as the transmission of discoveries of such universal principles (and the technologies derived from them). This leads immediately to a still-higher consideration. What is the means by which to promote the development of the ability to generate, replicate, and transmit those non-deductive ideas typified by experimentally valid discoveries of universal physical principles? A Classical humanist mode in education, as opposed to the mind-destroying educational policies presently rampant in U.S. schools and universities, and in today's "Flagellant"-like epidemic of socially induced video-games schizophrenia, is an example of the problem to be addressed for remedial action.

This means, that industrial progress requires an increase in the number of persons so employed, and also an upgrading of the average skill levels and standard of living of the households of the persons so employed. Other points exposing the fraud of the Malthusian theses will be touched upon in this report. At the present moment, the following points should be read as relevant to that conclusion.

This means, that a higher standard of living should be defined functionally, in terms of those physical and related changes which foster the increase of that human cognitive potential in the individual, family household, and community affairs, of society.

To realize the potential which cognitive discoveries represent for increasing potential relative population-density, we must, in effect, constantly change the Biosphere. Look at this matter within a context which takes us one step beyond Vernadsky's definition of the Noösphere.

This means improving nature in ways which raise the level of the Biosphere, such as causing deserts to bloom, placing water distribution under human management, increasing useful development of forests, fish farming, and so on. In these and other ways, we are helping the Biosphere to reach levels of anti-entropic development it could not achieve without human intervention. This includes applied foresight into managing our relationship to such matters as depletion of fossils of the Biosphere, such as atmosphere and water, such that we are efficiently offsetting our tendency to deplete those needed fossil reserves.

This also means, adding an accumulation of "fossils" of human cognitive activity, such as artefacts of man-needed technologies not otherwise available within the bounds of functions of the pre-existing Biosphere as such. Basic economic infrastructure devel-

---

8. In other words, rather than linear "activity analysis," we must progress to methods of approximation which imply a truly non-linear, e.g., Riemannian function, expressed by the question, "Tensors, anyone?" Tensors applicable to domains of the power of n+1 experimentally defined universal physical principles of action.

oped and maintained by government, is an example of this. Physical capital-intensity of investment in production, is another example of such man-generated fossils of the Noösphere.

The combination of such man-made improvements in the Biosphere and Noösphere, represents man's physical-economic relationship to his total environment. It is the ratio of man's level of scientific and technological development, to the results of such man-managed relationship to the man-altered Biosphere and Noösphere, which delimit, and otherwise determine the possible rate of improvement of the potential relative population-density of our species. The efforts required to maintain and improve that relationship, constitute the determinants of the potential productivity of the society, and, therefore, define the true costs of production for the society as a whole.

The individual place of employment is to be assessed solely in terms of its functional relationship to that relatively universal set of bounding conditions.

The determination of the outcome of the employment of the individual operative, is properly defined in those relatively universal terms of reference.

When this matter is examined competently, it is clear that technology, as such, does not "steal jobs"; technological progress as such requires a change in employment, from lower to higher quality of employment opportunities generally. Any different ultimate effect is not the result of technology, but of bad policy, or of bad management, of national governments, banking institutions, or firms.

Specifically, any increase in productivity effected through technological progress, results in an increase of the per-capita margin of anti-entropy in the physical-economic process as a whole, and therefore a potential increase in both the rate and quality of average employment available. If that progress does not occur, we must find the causes for that failure, in either general defects in prevalent popular culture, or the need to correct the prevalent mismanagement of important groups of enterprises, or of the society as a whole.

To achieve that growth, it is necessary to expand the labor-force, so as to assimilate efficiently a more complex division of labor, which means increasing the size of the population, by either expanding the number of births, increasing functional qualities of life-expectancies, or a combination of both, while raising the functional standard of living as development of the cognitive powers of the population requires this.

2. The Kautsky-Plekhanov Syndrome

There were two generic forms of systemic failures commonplace among so-called Marxist movements of the Twentieth Century. First, was that mechanistic misconception of social processes, which was associated with the quasi-Hegelian doctrine of "historical objectivity," typified by Karl Kautsky, G. Plekhanov, et al. This was opposed to the so-called "voluntarist" conception of history, the latter counterposed, among socialists, to Plekhanov's views, by V.I. Lenin and some others. The second, was the specific role attributed to the working-class by the apostles of "historical objectivity," the working-class portrayed as the cattle-like species which was presumed to secrete the juices of the transition to socialism.

The "historically objective" school based itself on a variant of the neo-Cathar thesis of Physiocrat François Quesnay. It accepted, as all empiricist and kindred currents did, the fatalistic notion of history, otherwise featured by G.W.F. Hegel, that the evolution of society is determined by mysterious forces operating mystically, "either from under the floorboards of, or outside the real universe." Marxists have often embraced this mystical faith in "objective history," as the process by which the capitalist "phase of" development of a working-class would, in due course, make the latter the virtual inheritor of history. It were then assumed to be the duty of a patiently waiting working-class political movement, to prepare for the day of "proletarian rapture," which would be delivered as soon as something akin to Hegel's world-spirit might sound the relevant tocsin.

Lenin's break with Plekhanov et al., is fascinating, not only because his allegedly un-Marxist, "voluntarist" doctrine was borne out in the fact of the 1917 revolutionary process in Russia. It is also significant still today, because of the way in which Lenin, who was poorly developed from the standpoint of scientific method generally, nonetheless captured the essence of scientific practice, in his commitment to a "voluntarist" approach to the shaping of history.

By voluntarism, one should not intend to suggest that merely arbitrary changes can be made in history. The argument is, simply, the same argument made by any competent scientific discoverer, that any valid principle, once discovered, can succeed, under the conditions in which its application is made feasible. Lenin's coup d'état of 1917 succeeded, despite all of the estab-

V.I. Lenin, though poorly developed from the standpoint of scientific method generally, nonetheless captured the essence of scientific practice, in his commitment to a "voluntarist" approach to the shaping of history.

lished Russian reform parties, and virtually despite the Bolshevik party, too. It succeeded, because, as he had foreseen and understood, no competing, existing or foreseeable party of Russia, was then prepared to take the one course of action which would save Russia from virtual Hell: pull Russia unilaterally out of the hopeless war which had already been lost.[9] It was the systemic failure of all those parties which, in effect, left the possibility of a continued existence of Russia to the only leadership on the ground, Lenin's, which was able to provide any basis at all for the continued existence of Russia during the generation ahead.

Relatively speaking, Lenin was right. However, although Lenin emphasized Soviet Russia's need to adopt American methods, he, like the Marxists generally, otherwise missed the points essential for the continued viable existence of Russia in the longer term, the lesson of the American Revolution, to which I shall turn a bit

---

9. Notable is Lenin's overriding L. Trotsky et al. on the matter of the Brest-Litovsk peace.

later in this report. In short, that portion of the history of Russia, and the case of Lenin, are typical of real history, which almost invariably mocks all utopian systems of thought, "orthodox Marxism" included.

More recently, over more than forty years of recent history, there has been an almost global collapse of the "idea of socialism" in its more or less traditional "Marxist" form. This demoralization of socialists generally, emerged over the course of the interval of the Khrushchev leadership in the Soviet Union. However, if we examine matters more closely, we must recognize that the relevant errors of the socialist movement, were chiefly reflections of the same ideological decadence which had been spread, up to the present moment, from the so-called British and French "Enlightenment" of the Eighteenth Century.

It was Marx's and others' error, of situating their definition of socialism as a proposed alternative and successor to the British empiricist's definition of "capitalism;" and that, within the bounds of British economic mythology, which led more and more of the Soviet leadership, in particular, back to intellectual convergence upon radically empiricist currents of British liberal ideology. By defining "socialism," from the start, as the historically fated outcome of developments from within British political-economy, the failures of socialist doctrine, so induced, produced the subsequent failures which led socialist ideologues back to reconciliation with their adopted Benthamite liberal roots.

It was, as I have emphasized above, Marx's refusal to accept the lessons of the exceptional role of the American Revolution in world history, which, combined with his mistaken enthusiasms for the Enlightenment, typify the errors, and resulting practical failures, incurred by Marxian and related socialist doctrines.

It is notable, on this account, that the defects in the economic and related doctrines of Karl Marx, reflect the influence of the axiomatic Romanticism of that "Enlightenment," as opposed to the Classical humanist influences expressed in Benjamin Franklin's role, in shaping the American Revolution's character and policies according to the anti-Locke conceptions of Gottfried Leibniz et al.

In economics, Marx's errors, such as his failure to grasp the actual significance of Minister Jean-Baptiste Colbert, and his misreading of the schema of Quesnay, together with his misguided enthusiasm for the alleged "scientific" qualities of the related influences of British East India Company ideologues such as Adam Smith,

Jeremy Bentham, and David Ricardo, are of crucial significance. His exclusion of the actual development of the modern sovereign nation-state economy, accounts for his tendency toward those mystical aberrations to which I refer under the rubric of "historical objectivity."

The characteristics of the recent decades' degeneration of the modern economies of the United States and Europe, from relatively successful producer societies, to decadent, degenerating consumer societies, since the assassination of U.S. President Kennedy, also illuminates the relevant, axiomatic features of Marx's credulity respecting the Eighteenth and Nineteenth centuries' British political-economy.

In the Bigger Picture

As I have indicated above, Lenin missed the larger point, but proceeded by a slightly different route than Marx before him. In the main, he was a practicing Marxist, but he also took a detour of somewhat crucial historical significance for today.

As measured in demographic results, the emergence of modern European civilization, during the Fifteenth-Century Renaissance, has been the greatest leap forward in the known history of mankind.

Since that Renaissance, the characteristic defects in inherited from earlier periods of that civilization, have always been, chiefly, reflections of the cultural heritage of ancient imperial Rome and Babylon earlier. That is the Roman cultural heritage which has sought to destroy modern civilization in its infancy, as during the Venice-directed Habsburg-led religious warfare of the 1511-1648 interval. It is that heritage, which is expressed, again, subsequent to 1648, by the effort led by the Anglo-Dutch liberalism of Venice's Paolo Sarpi, to parasitize those impulses of modern civilization which it could not yet prevent. The recurring tendency has been, periodically, to turn the clock of progress backward, in a way which parodies the way in which the Rome emerging from the period of the Second Punic War. The result has become, during the recent thirty-odd years, a parody of the decadent, parasitical form of consumer society known as imperial Rome.

Contrary to the Marxists generally, and also Lenin in particular, the British economy under the control of the Anglo-Dutch India companies, was not a national agro-industrial economy which also happened, as an afterthought, to adopt a Romantic form of imperialism as a supplementary feature. To restate this crucial point,

review the issues of that observation, very briefly, as follows.

In what passed for "orthodox Marxism," the doctrine was the following. It was supposed that the so-called "capitalist" economy of the British isles, was a lawful "stage" of historical political-economic development. It was argued, that this national economy acquired the added attribute of imperialism.

The truth was exactly the reverse.

From the time of George I and Walpole's liberalism, the British economy of Adam Smith et al., came into existence as, and was always primarily an imperial parasite in more or less conscious imitation of the Roman Empire. It was, predominantly, a consumer society with sundry, subordinated, domestic agro-industrial features. Until a shift which occurred during the Twentieth Century, the United Kingdom's domestic policy was carefully managed under what remained, in fact, a strongly protectionist screen against unwanted intrusions. Yet, then as now, the objective was always a lust for "invisible earnings" from abroad, chiefly those pilfered by "Artful Dodger" Adam Smith's "invisible hand."[10] On this latter point, Rosa Luxemburg's emphasis on the characteristic role of international loans, as that of Herbert Feis, was right, relative to Lenin and the Social Democrats.

In fact, the British Eighteenth-Century economy was an outgrowth of the preceding, centuries-long role of Venice as the leading imperial maritime power of the Mediterranean region, Europe included. In its effort to reverse the revolutionary successes of the Fifteenth-Century Renaissance, Venice's ruling rentier-financier class used its Habsburg assets, based in Austria and Spain, to drown Europe in religious warfare, as the characteristic feature of the 1511-1648 interval. In this process, over the course of the Seventeenth and early Eighteenth centuries, the Venetians developed the Netherlands and England as bases of a neo-Venetian imperial maritime power, the Dutch and British India companies of William of Orange and Lord Shelburne typify the neo-Venetian form of the Dutch and British monarchies, with the Dutch being subordinated to the British during the course of the early Eighteenth Century.

_____

10. The important component of the change, was the effect of the dominant role of the U.S. in the British Empire's economy over the course of two World Wars and their late Twentieth-Century aftermath. The disgusting case of the first government of Prime Minister Harold Wilson, typifies that continuing process of degeneration.

Thus, contrary to the Marxist and kindred myths, from the beginning, these monarchies and their political-economic systems were imperialist in character. The domestic aspects of those economies were developed as the always subordinated instruments of the imperial rentier-financier power. Their consciously adopted model, especially for the British monarchy, was the ancient Roman Empire as it developed out of the processes unleashed in the course and aftermath of the Second Punic War. The Eighteenth-Century control of the British monarchy by the East India Company, as best typified by the role of Shelburne, expresses the essential features of the British monarchy, from both its roots under the bloody tyranny of William of Orange and with the seating of the Hanoverian dynasty in 1714.

One can not understand anything essential about modern European history, without recognizing the distinction between that revolutionary impulse expressed by the Fifteenth-Century Renaissance, and the emergence of what became, in effect, Anglo-Dutch liberalism. This liberal regime's relationship to the impact of the Classical Renaissance, mimicked the parasitical relationship of imperial Rome to the Classical legacy best expressed by Platonic Greece.

Since the Congress of Vienna, the British Empire and that feudal tradition associated with the legacy of the Holy Alliance, have been both bloody rivals, and, also, as John Quincy Adams knewm, and the U.S. Civil War illustrates, the mortal enemy of the system defined by the U.S. Declaration of Independence and Federal Constitution.

Thus, world history since the death of U.S. President Franklin Roosevelt, has been shaped chiefly by the effort of a neo-Romantic, essentially parasitical, dominant political-economic class, a class whose interests and methods are a continuation of the Venetian imperial maritime legacy. The maritime wars between the British and Netherlands, and Britain's insistence on its role as the world's only maritime superpower, up through the aftermath of World War I, expresses the Venetian character of the London oligarchy. Since the successful 1901 assassination of U.S. President William McKinley, the continuing strategic outlook of the English-speaking imperial financier oligarchy, has been the emphasis, initially, on maritime, and then also aerial supremacy, as leading strategic instruments of intended global imperial rule.

Since 1901, the continued commitment of the Anglo-American financier oligarchy, has been the effort to use, but also contain and destroy the continuing impulse of the American System of political-economy, while bringing the entire world, step by step, under the "eternal" rule of an English-speaking parody of ancient imperial Rome. The death of Franklin Roosevelt, was taken as the opportunity to bring such a world empire into being, step-wise.

The Takeover
That characteristic impulse and trend of the 1945-2002 interval, has passed through two successive phases.

In the first phase, from the death of Franklin Roosevelt, until the aftermath of the assassination of President Kennedy, the post-Roosevelt U.S., together with Europe, remained a producer society, but controlled increasingly by a class which sat upon and exploited the productive forces it required for building up and maintaining its power, as had the British monarchy during certain phases of its existence.

In the second phase, from about the beginning of the neo-feudalist U.S. Indo-China war, a precipitous, now thirty-seven-year shift from a producer society, to a consumer society, was imposed upon both the Americas and Europe. These impulses were a reflection of the already characteristic feature of economy under the British monarchy, from the accession of George I to the present day.[11]

Here, in that second phase, we see the hand of the Luddite myth. The recurring, pro-Malthusian impulse of the system of the British monarchy, has always been to prevent that Classical impulse of the Fifteenth-Century Renaissance, on which the superior power of modern European civilization depended, from securing governing power in its own name and interest. The British monarchy's targetted foe, was the interest expressed, typically, by the American System of political-economy.

The natural outgrowth of that struggle to subdue the Classical impulse, has always been expressed, since the struggle for independence of the United States by hatred directed against what today's fascists and kindred types denounce as "American exceptionalism." The liberal

---

11. Marx's view of the economy under that British monarchy's rule, often missed the recurring impulse of that monarchy, to suffocate the baby and enthrone the afterbirth.

FAO

"Technology, as such, does not 'steal jobs'; technological progress as such requires a change in employment, from lower to higher quality of employment opportunities generally. Any different ultimate effect is not the result of technology, but of bad policy, or of bad management, of national governments, banking institutions, or firms." Here, jobs are provided, but at the lowest possible technological level, as peasants in Bangladesh carry loads of earth in baskets in an attempt to restore canals destroyed by flooding.

form of economy built up under the British monarchy already had that Romantic characteristic. Marx was the victim of his British indoctrination to that effect, a weakness in Marx which was repeatedly reenforced in him by Frederick Engels' interventions against Marx's recurring leaning toward the economics of Friedrich List, earlier, and Henry C. Carey, later.

The Malthusian and related Luddite eruptions within British ideology, must be so situated within that context. (I must here refer, once again, to the wildly gnostic mysticism underlying "free trade" dogma, as has been unavoidable in numerous locations published earlier. Yet, since the disease of "free trade" persists, so must the relevant medication.)

Within that context, the quasi-Darwinian idea of a pulsation of "objective" evolutionary forces of history, as a specifically empiricist trait assimilated into Marx's own writings, has its principal specific origin in the founding of modern empiricism by Venice's Paolo Sarpi. Within Sarpi's neo-Ockhamite dogma, there is embedded the type of neo-manichean mysticism spread

throughout Europe, by such influences as the still-active Cathar legacy within significant circles of France today. It was this same hybrid of Cathar-empiricist legacies, which produced the *laissez-faire* mysticism of Quesnay, and which permeated the thinking of all of those British East India Company empiricists who influenced the thinking of Marx, and, more emphatically, Frederick "Opposable Thumb" Engels, on both the origins of political-economy and the nature of scientific method.

The common religious fanaticism shared among the empiricists and related Enlightenment figures such as neo-Cathar Quesnay, is the implicit, or stated assumption, that everything known to man, but one, is located within the bounds of sense-certainty. The exception is an agency external to the sense-perceived universe, which exerts an arbitrary influence on the throw of the dice, by means of which some men are magically made rich, and others rendered destitute, or, simply, dead. The gnostic versions of this presume, that a magical relationship can be established between the believer and that supernatural, arbitrary influence, lurking, so to speak, under the floorboards of the universe.

Such are the pseudo-Christian, gnostic beliefs of those lunatic heathen, known as "Christian Zionists," who insist, that by acting to bring about a Battle of Armageddon, they can force God, as if by magic spells, to bring on what those gnostics term "The Rapture." The popularity of gambling in U.S. churches, and other circles, reflects the same heathen quality of gnostic superstition. The popularity of the dogmas of "free trade" and "new economy," are systemically consistent with the gnostic characteristics of the "Christian Zionist" variety of contemporary heathen.

This was the gnostic religious dogma of the Cathars. It was the gnostic dogma of Thomas Hobbes, John

Locke, Bernard Mandeville, and British East India Company ideologues such as Adam Smith, Jeremy Bentham, and David Ricardo. It was the essence of that doctrine of *laissez-faire* which the British copied from the Physiocrats under the name of "free trade." This same gnostic superstition was widely imitated among so-called Marxists, as the underlying axiomatic assumption of the empiricist doctrine of historical determinism, as the "anti-voluntarist" superstition called "historical objectivity."

Such was the specific influence of the Eighteenth-Century, British and French Enlightenment on Marx and the Marxists. Such was the origin of the dogma of "historical objectivity" adopted by Kautsky and Plekhanov, among others, and influential among non-Marxist trade-unionists ideologically infected from similar sources.

For related reasons, the socialists, in general, never understood capitalism. Their first error, on this account, was their acceptance of the delusion to which I have referred above, that the development of modern national economy developed first under the British monarchy. They assumed, therefore, that the successful form of modern society was rooted in that misanthropic perversion which Marx was induced to call by the name of "capitalism."

It did not occur to Marx, or to the socialists generally, that the first modern nation-state economies appeared during the Fifteenth Century, first in Louis XI's France, and, after that, Henry VII's England. Similarly, Marx et al. refused to face the fact, that the first science of political-economy was developed by Gottfried Leibniz, over the interval 1671-1716, and that the first successful form of modern, post-1648 national economy was developed, largely, under the influence of Leibniz's work spread into North America. The result of Leibniz's and related influences on North America, was what U.S. Treasury Secretary Alexander Hamilton, among others, described as the American System of political-economy, and what List and Carey treated as national economy.

For reason of the influence of British ideology, on Marx and others, the predominantly mythical image of British "capitalism," also spread among the socialists generally. Most socialists, especially those rooted in ideas of "historical objectivity," were never able to understand several most crucial of the problematic, systemic features of real modern economies, including both the U.S. economy and the problems of the Soviet system.

3. Modern National Economy

A systemically viable form of the economy of a modern nation-state republic, has three economic pillars.

The first of these, is the economic function of the state, expressed in the state's unique responsibility for developing and maintaining both "hard" and "soft" aspects of basic economic infrastructure. The second is the role of the technologically innovative private entrepreneur, who relies directly, or indirectly, on discoveries of experimentally valid universal principles, and also depends upon the state's regulation, fostering, and protection of those functions. The third is the production and injection of those scientific and related discoveries on which the continued, long-range viability of the national economy depends.

These three principles, are bound together by a single, twofold principle of constitutional law: the interdependent conceptions of perfect national sovereignty and the ancient Platonic/Christian principle called *agapē* in the Classical Greek, and identified in modern English-language usage by the terms "general welfare" or "common good." The system of national credit-creation, inhering in the principle of perfect sovereignty, performs a crucial function in the organizing of economic growth, and recoveries from the follies of economic depressions.

These elements, so combined, constitute a national economy, absolutely distinct from either socialist or British ideological definitions of "capitalist" economies. These combined elements typify the American System of national economy, as Alexander Hamilton, the Careys, and Friedrich List described it. To understand the exceptional economic and related potential of such a form of national economy, relative to all others. we must often focus upon the functional interconnection among those component aspects.

These features were already axiomatically characteristic of France under Louis XI and the England of Henry VII and Sir Thomas More. Those precedents have been obscured from general and even academic opinion, that more or less successfully, by the bloody spectacle of the Habsburg-centered, feudal reaction, in conducting the virtual "new dark age" of simmering or actual religious wars, which dominated the 1511-1648 interval of European history. Thus, the usual vision of the internal characteristics of modern European history, does not reach earlier than the 1648 Treaty of Westphalia. Many erroneous assumptions prevalent even among professionals today, are based on short-sighted opinions of that, or even much more impoverished views of modern history.

The modern sovereign nation-state economy, is the first known form of society in which the mass of the population was not degraded juridically, in law and practice, to the status of human cattle. The doctrine of John Locke is typical of the notions of law invoked in defense of the institution of slavery and kindred forms of degradation of the mass of the population to human cattle-like conditions. The contemporary pro-fascist doctrine of "shareholder value" by avowed "textualist" U.S. Justice Antonin Scalia, is a radically positivist reading of Locke, copied out of the Preamble to the Constitution of the Confederate States of America, and carried to a dictionary nominalist's extreme.

The principle of the sovereign nation-state republic could not be restated too often these days. The presently imperilled United States will not outlive the present world monetary-financial crisis, unless we restore the principle, that the moral authority of the government to rule, is conditional upon that sovereign's efficient promotion of the general welfare of all of the living population and its posterity.

This principle defines the modern sovereign nation-state as the first known form of society in which the first, controlling self-interest of the government, is to meet the requirements of maintaining and uplifting the demographic characteristics of the population as a whole. In all other forms of society, including a society ordered according to Scalia's perverted conception, that of "shareholder value," the majority of the population is degraded, juridically, and in practice, to the condition of human cattle, to be disposed of at the pleasure of those who hold title to the greater portion of "shareholder interest."

Contrast the sovereign nation-state with the situation of the so-called citizens of the Roman Empire.

The Roman Empire was ruled by the popular opinion of the citizens, but the citizens were nothing better than human cattle. Earlier, we have the case of the judicial murder of Socrates, by the democratic party of Athens, which warns us against reliance on current fads in popular opinion. Democracy is, therefore, not the standard of a republic. Rather, the *willful* realization of the general welfare of the people must rule. In effect, the individual citizen of the sovereign nation-state republic, is bound by obligations to the entire population, and to the future population, not merely his own "democratic" preference.

The apparently paradoxical implications of that argument, is that the ruling principle of law and policy of a true republic is the principle of *truthfulness*. Without a principle of truthfulness, there can be no true law of a sovereign republic. Without a ruling, Socratic standard of truth, a would-be republic degenerates into something like the ultimately self-doomed, evil Empire of Rome, as the U.S. and its population have been degenerating, morally and economically, during the recent thirty-odd years. It is exactly that specific sort of moral rot, which is the efficient agency of the immediate threat of self-destruction of our nation.

This standard of truth has two phases. One of these might be identified as "the bottom line." *What is the result which defines a truthful performance by the nation?* The second is represented by the choice of policy, that intention, by means of which the required outcome is efficiently ordered. *By the standard represented by long-range economic cycles, what policies will achieve a general increase of the potential relative population-density of the whole population and its posterity?*

That, however, does not signify a hedonistic standard, such as the hedonistic standard (the so-called hedonistic principle) defined by the utterly depraved Jeremy Bentham, or the hedonistic standard expressed by the utterly depraved "Quality Adjustment Index" of today's U.S. Government and Federal Reserve System. It does involve tangible results, but, like all experimentally valid notions of universal physical principles, these are defined as means to an end, not as an end in and of themselves. The "bottom line" is both the cognitive quality of moral development of the character of the individual person, and the provision of physical conditions and means consistent with the promotion and expression of that moral development.

'Agapē' as an Economic Principle

The perpetuation and improvement of the general welfare, signifies the production and development of individual persons qualified, motivated, and situated, to increase the power of the human species in and over the universe we are implicitly entrusted to manage and develop.

This is a concept associated with the use of the term *agapē* by Plato, as that same meaning is underlined by the Christian Apostle Paul in **I Corinthians** 13, in

Paul's condemnation of the substitution of a set of "single issue" rules of behavior for goodness. That term, *agapē*, is what is echoed by the terms general welfare, or common good. The essential interest of every person is *to do good*, in that specific sense, as Cotton Mather and Benjamin Franklin emphasized that notion. That notion of *agapē*, so expressed, is the moral essence of the founding of the American System of political-economy, the American System of national economy. That is the quality which the enemies of the founding of our republic hate, and seek to extirpate even from the memory of future humanity.

The notion of *agapē* arose in the dialogues of Plato as a complement to the Socratic notion of the immortality of the human soul, as that notion was later placed famously at the center of the German Eighteenth-Century Classical renaissance, by Moses Mendelssohn.

The term *agapē*, sometimes translated as *caritas* or *charity*, signifies love of the soul of the other, and also one's own. This notion is inseparable from what modern European civilization came to recognize as the process of discovery of universal physical principles, and the related process of generating those experiences of beauty associated with Classical principles of artistic composition and performance. This cognitive development of the human individual, and of the powers of that individual, is what we love. It is the realization of that kind of potential, within ourselves and within others, which we should love. It is, therefore, the uplifting of the meanest and most deprived persons in terms of those potentials of their nature, which has a special power to move us to the tears of joy implied in **I Corinthians** 13.

These represent efficient physical principles. It is through the development of the cognitive powers associated with experimentally valid universal physical principles, that mankind's existence in the universe, is not only increased, but the continuation of humanity defended against the forces of attrition. It is through the development of the individual character through forms best typified by principles of Classical artistic composition, that persons are organized around the discovery, development, and use of those universal physical principles upon which the maintenance and improvement of potential relative population-density depend absolutely.

Such are the interchangeable proper meanings of *agapē love*, the *general welfare*, and the *common good*.

To grasp the sense of sheer horror, of the presence of evil, which a Luddite or Malthusian sentiment should evoke in any moral human being, look at the horrid implications of the denial of access, by a child or adolescent in modern society, to a Classical humanist mode of education.

"Classical humanist education," should be freely translated as "the only policy of an education fit for human beings." This means, that education is focussed upon that principle which distinguishes a person from all other forms of life. This is the principle of cognition, as distinct from mere deductive learning of text; this is the principle of hypothesis, by means of which individual human minds have been able to accomplish what no other form of life can do: discover an experimentally valid universal physical principle.

Without the social realization of the fruits of that principle, the human species could never have achieved a total population of much more than several millions ape-like individuals, on the entirety of this planet, under the variable conditions existing on this planet during the recent two million years. The growth of the human population has been the combined effect of both the discovery and the transmission of such discoveries of principle, not only among contemporaries, but over successive generations. It is that combined process of individual discovery and transmission of experimentally valid universal principles, which is the crucial feature of all valid aspects of the development and persistence of human cultures.

Thus, the strategic economic necessity for education, can be efficiently served only by a policy of education which is based on the replication of individual cognitive acts of valid hypothesizing, among the members of society, especially in the educational experience of the new members of society. That is the basis for defining a Classical humanist education, as distinct from the animal-like educational policies practiced increasingly in schools and universities under the influence of the change of the economies of Europe and the Americas, from producer societies, to decadent consumer societies.

The subsuming feature of a Classical humanist education, is not simply the transmission of particular knowledge of principles, but, rather, the development of the personal moral character of the pupil. By "moral character," we Classical humanists signify a controlling sense of the different notion of individual self-interest, which separates the bestial impulses of sense-certainty from the location of the sense of personal identity in a notion of being a cognitive, social individual.

I have often illustrated that point of distinction, by pointing to the image of a pupil reenacting a discovery of universal principle by Archimedes. The pupil is not only reenacting the cognitive form of the mental act of hypothesizing used by Archimedes; the pupil is bringing that act to life within the pupil's own living mental processes. Repeated experiences of this quality, afford the pupil a sense of a relatively immortal quality of historical identity of the human individual. Archimedes is not a dead man; he is a good neighbor, a wise living uncle, a living presence inside oneself.

Thus, do we identify important discoveries of principle by the personal names of known original, or putatively original discoverers. Thus, the notion of efficient truth, in physical science and other matters, becomes, for the student in a Classical humanist education, a comprehensible notion of moral value. It is upon the fostering of this in the young, that we best produce new generations of adult populations capable of being true, sane, morally responsible citizens of a true republic.

This sense of cognitive connections to past and future generations, and from one current of culture to another, presents the developing young individual with a notion of the meaning of being human, of being a cognitive being, rather than just another beast putting its snout into subjects of sense-certainty. It is the love of being human, defined in this way, which affords the educated young citizen an efficient, practical comprehension of the standard for defining a notion of the general welfare.

It is that notion of the general welfare, which defines the required economic and related policies of a nation.

The Entrepreneur

The term "entrepreneur" should be read here and now in a way consistent with the German use of *Mittelstand*. This distinguishes the entrepreneur from the impersonal joint-stock corporation. This entrepreneur is not primarily motivated by the desire to earn an income; he, or she seeks to carry out a chosen mission in a way which he or she believes will also provide the income and other resources needed both to conduct that mission, and hopefully to pass the same kind of opportunity to others who may succeed him. That is the fundamental moral difference between the true entrepreneur and today's image of the predatory stockholder of a "shareholder interest."

It is that quality of entrepreneur which represents an essential characteristic of a modern national economy of the type the U.S. was founded to become. Since such entrepreneurs are essential for durable forms of progress of the economy as a whole, and since they are indi-

vidually vulnerable to attacks by predators and other aversive circumstances, it is the moral obligation, and self-interest of the nation to provide such individual entrepreneurs, such as our progressive farmers, a certain protection. We therefore oblige the stock-corporation to imitate the entrepreneur, and regulate the environment of such corporations to that intended effect.

To such included purposes, and for the general welfare otherwise, the state is obliged to provide the basic economic infrastructure, which represents the economic environment, including the maintenance of the Biosphere, on which the effective functioning of the entrepreneurs depends.

Since, however, all economic progress depends upon relatively high rates of scientific and technological progress, all successful national economies are also, more or less emphatically, science-driver economies. It is from the fostering of scientific progress, that the spill-over of the development of technologies into the work of the entrepreneur occurs. Here, again, the function of Classical humanist education comes to the fore. Without the equivalent of the effect of a Classical humanist mode in education, significant progress were not likely; without a general development of the population in that same way, the ability of the general population to sustain scientific and technological progress would tend to be marginal.

In the totality of the division of productive labor within a national economy, the greater portion must be assigned either to the economic activity of government, or to private investment in forms of public utilities which are regulated by the national, regional or community governments. This portion of the total economic output pertains chiefly, by its nature to economic measures necessary to maintenance of the productive potential of the land-area as a whole, or the population as a whole. These tasks are, by their nature, ill-suited for private ownership.

This basic economic infrastructure is the foundation on which private ownership of an individual enterprise sits, as the superstructure of a building sits upon its foundations.

There are admissible exceptions to that rule of division of responsibility, but the exceptions should be made in cases and ways in which the purpose of the rule is served.

The essential character of the relationship between those public and private forms of enterprise is most simply illustrated, by reducing the functional relationship to the pedagogical form of an hypothetical case.

Given two virtually identical entrepreneurships, in two different national economies, or differently maintained regions of the same economy. Let the technologies, skills, and efficiencies, and qualities of products in the compared cases be virtually the same. Let the same management direct both, according to consistent policies and practices. There will often be even very significant differences between the productivities of the compared enterprises. The principal cause of those differences will be the combined effect of a different state of development of basic economic infrastructure, and differences in policies of practice of government in the respective areas. Transportation, power, education, popular artistic and related culture, and health-care, are typical of the major factors determining those differences.

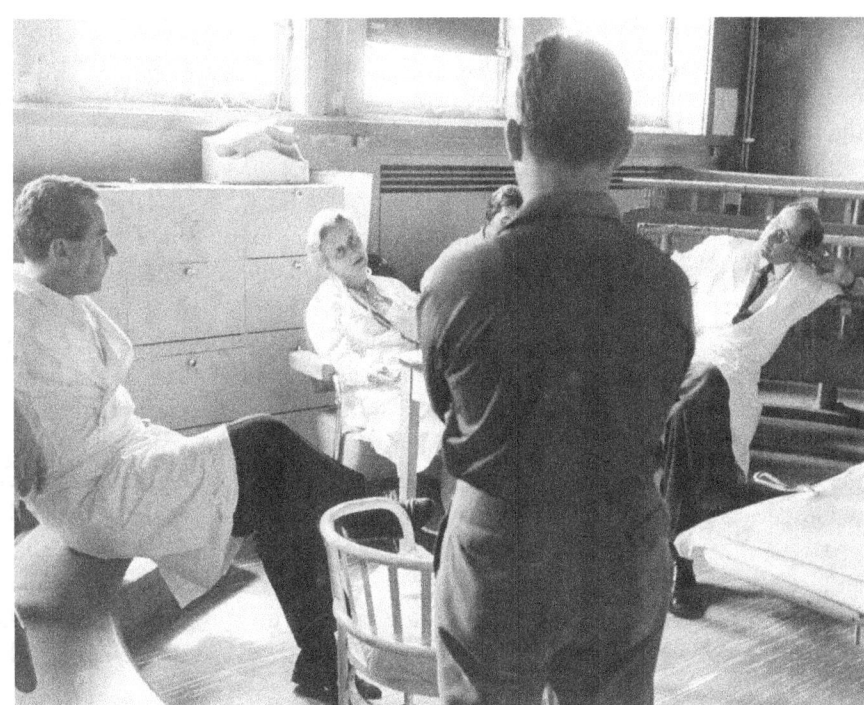
WHO

"In the case of medicine, it is the treatment of the patient, not an accountant's standardized definition of disease and allowed treatments, which is the standard for ethical practice." Here, a medical team deliberates on the treatment of a cancer patient.

For that and related reasons, there is a corresponding proper division of assigned economic responsibility of government and private enterprise, for maintaining and improving the average productive powers of labor of the national economy. The constitutional regulatory functions of good government, under the principle of the general welfare, obliges the stockholder-owned corporation to meet the same general standard of policy typical of the healthy entrepreneurship.

That stated, now ask yourself: Why is that division of responsibility desirable, even necessary for a healthy national economy? The answer for this lies where the typical Marxist, or anarcho-syndicalist, would frantically deny it to exist. This difference in opinion is, in fact, the chief social reason that socialist economies tend to relative failures of performance.

The quality of the technologically successful entrepreneur, is a reflection of the development of his or her cognitive powers in a way akin to the practice of a creatively productive scientist, or physician. When this principle, common to those various cases, is not recognized, the result will tend to be akin to the murderous folly produced by increasingly mechanized standards which the unfolding of the foolish HMO act has produced, in creating what is in fact a cruel malpractice of

medicine by accountants and financial officers. In the case of medicine, it is the treatment of the patient, not an accountant's standardized definition of disease and allowed treatments, which is the standard for ethical practice. *The principle which underlies these various types of cases, is the fact, that those kinds of developed cognitive powers, by means of which experimentally valid universal physical principles are discovered, is a sovereign act of the individual mind, an action whose expression is perfectly opaque to the sense-perceptual powers of an observer, or instrument substituted for an observer.* The qualifying distinction of the indicated type of entrepreneur, such as the machine-tool design specialist, is of that nature.

This argument does not imply that creative professionalism and the like does not occur within the government-directed infrastructure program. The point is, that the relative freedom of expression afforded the class of creative entrepreneurs, is precious for its unique contribution to the progress of the economy as a whole. Not accidentally, such entrepreneurships may have been impelled to take up that career out of frustration with the cumbersome, bureaucratized practices of the public-stock-owned, or "Wall Street"-controlled enterprise.

This function of the entrepreneur is not limited to the distinguishable entrepreneur himself. It is the quality which that entrepreneur will often foster among his or her employees, especially the most trusted ones. It is the proliferation of that quality of creative performance within the pores of the private sector of the economy, which was the famous source of the former "miracles" of production of the U.S. economy, and of, for example, German industry, or the strongest features of entrepreneurship in regions of Italy today.

The principle here is what I have identified, above, as the "voluntarist" principle, against which the "orthodox Marxists" railed, as do the foolish followers of Adam Smith, to the present day. The object is to foster the development of as high a percentile of "voluntarist" personalities as possible within the pores of the social process. This mission features the development of the small entrepreneurship, usually of not more than 100-200 employees, often of a few, as in the case of the high-technology family farm, as the cutting edge of progress in the economy.

This is not only a needed economic policy. It is also social-political policy. A healthy republic requires not only well-educated young minds. It requires a population with cognitively active minds. To achieve that effect, this social-political policy must be fostered in the daily, weekly workplace, a location in which much of the daily life and energy of the adult citizen is occupied.

Now, to sum up the argument against the Luddites, before turning to the concluding arguments of this report.

The source of all increases in the productive powers of labor, is the combined effect of introducing experimentally valid universal physical principles, and the cultural development which fosters cooperation in the utilization of those principles and the technologies derived from them. The ability to expand the application of existing technologies, and to introduce new ones, requires medium- to-long-term advances in investment, after which the benefit is harvested gradually. The source of the credit for such investment in that future harvest, must come ultimately from a crucial margin of new credit, outside any current deposits of monetary wealth. This can come only from the sovereign debt-capacity of the nation-state, which through its monopoly on the emission of currency and power to commit itself to such issues in advance, is able to strike the balance between present and future investments and harvests, which fosters what is called "full employment."

This margin of state-created credit, since the state incurs a debt in this way, must have reasonable security,

on the average, in the future harvest. Therefore, science-driver programs and expansion in the area of basic economic infrastructure, are the preferred choices for stimulating a growth of total employment.

This system works, if there is an increase in the average physically defined productive powers of labor, under which condition the debt-credit role of the nation-state is not counterinflationary. Thus, what are called "labor-saving" technologies, create more jobs than they supersede, if the nation approaches this matter intelligently.

However, the typical Luddite is usually a person of a serf mentality, who thinks, as a cow might think, I do what my father did before me. To the Luddite, a change in quality of occupation, is a threat to his estimation of his self-interest as a cow might define the security of her employment at the dairy. The bestialized person abhors change in his or her habituated, cattle-like behavior.

Economy, Education, and Utopia

For both economic and social-political reasons, a healthy national economy requires a universal standard of public and higher education of the Classical humanist form. The student's accumulation of experience of the act of original discovery of experimentally valid universal physical principles, is necessary for fostering those qualities of citizenship which are indispensable for the healthy functioning of a democratic republic. The study of the history of Classical principles of artistic composition in the same way, must be included, or the matriculated populations will tend to be morally, intellectually, and politically defective, on that account. This Classical-humanist reexperiencing of science and Classical art, provides the foundation for a rational comprehension of history from a cognitive standpoint. The matured young individual so educated, will meet the requirements of a qualified citizen of a republic.

These qualities, fostered in education, and in the generality of economic practice, are necessary for strategic reasons, as well as economic and political affairs of the nation. The task-orientation of a population so educated and employed, is indispensable for producing and maintaining the quality of citizen capable of resisting the kind of decadence which has rotted out transatlantic civilization since the retirement of President Eisenhower and assassination of President Kennedy.

Knowledge and practice can not, and must not be separated. We must have a science-driver form of national economy, not only to meet our material requirements, but to give an appropriate form of task-orientation to the mental life of our citizenry.

However, powerful transatlantic financial and related interests have been operating for decades on the basis of a directly contrary intention. The pro-Malthusian turn launched on behalf of "post-industrial society" during the second half of the 1960s, and the launching of the popular "ecology" movement at the beginning of the 1970s, are the root of the transformation of the U.S. and other economies from the growing post-war producer societies of the 1945-1965 interval, into the bankrupt world monetary-financial system of today.

Look at the "new Luddism" of the past thirty-five years, in light of what I had written above, on the relationship between education and economy.

Looking back at the 1961-1965 convulsions, in the U.S.A., Europe, and elsewhere, preceding the U.S. deep plunge into the Indo-China war, we see a massive destruction of the minds of the university students of the 1968 generation, a destruction based on sundry expressions of rabidly existentialist follies and a general economic-cultural paradigm-shift toward what has become, for today's adolescents, a "no-future" society. The characteristic feature of this cultural paradigm-shift, was an axiomatic change in the moral character of the U.S. and of European nations, from producer societies, to the decadence of consumer society.

The lack of a productive orientation for the two younger adult generations, the "Baby Boomers" and their progeny, has fostered a widespread and deepening moral and intellectual decadence, akin to that which plunged imperial Rome into a self-imposed Dark Age of European culture.

Not only is a science-driven producer society needed for the present economic requirements of humanity at large. Without a task-orientation of that type as the adopted form of national practice and goals, there will be a failure in the moral development of national populations, out of which such horrors as a plunge into a prolonged dark age of neo-Romantic universal fascism, were presently likely.

Precisely such a new dark age, has been the stated goal of utopians such as H.G. Wells, Bertrand Russell, and their numerous confederates, then, and among presently influential strategic utopians still today.[12] In order to bring about a world empire which eliminates the existence of sovereign nation-states, the population of powerful nation-states must be sufficiently ruined and "dumbed down," to accept what is in fact the status of a bred and culled human herd, as Wells proposed in 1928.

The British had done that to their own population, during the age of Walpole, and in the Benthamites' response to the threat from British sympathizers of the American Revolution. This had been the depraved state of British culture to which Babbage, Herschel, and Peacock had referred early during the Nineteenth Century. At the close of World War I, especially after the revival of the U.S. under President Franklin Roosevelt, this was already the relevant intention of certain very influential circles in Britain.

Near the beginning of the Twentieth Century, the Fabian circles, known as the Coefficients and Round Table, gathered around Lord Milner, Halford Mackinder, Wells, et al., represented circles associated with the Prince of Wales and later Edward VII, which had reacted with fear and loathing to President Lincoln's victory over the Anglo-French asset, the Confederacy. That fear increased with the spread of the influence of the American System of political-economy into Germany, Russia, Japan, and elsewhere, during the closing years of the 1870s. Britain saw the building prospect of a trans-Eurasian system of economic development based on American principles, as a mortal form of systemic threat to the supremacy of the British Empire as a neo-Venetian form of imperial maritime power. The British intention was to organize a fratricidal war among the principal powers of Eurasia, as a "geopolitical" strategy for stopping the spread of the American System's growing global influence. As we know, the trick succeeded.

Several preliminary steps in building toward that war, are notable here. The war began with British monarchy's takeover of the Emperor of Japan, launching the successive Japan wars against China, Korea, and Russia, during the 1894-1905 interval. Meanwhile, the successful 1901 assassination of U.S. President William McKinley, shifted the power in the U.S. to the pro-Confederacy circles typified by the Presidencies of Theodore Roosevelt and Ku Klux Klan fanatic Woodrow Wilson, and brought the United States into alliance with Britain for the coming World War. To "finish the job" which Versailles left uncompleted, the British monarchy, acting with the support of those New York banking circles which had been associated with Theo-

---

12. H.G. Wells, **The Open Conspiracy: Blueprints for a World Revolution** (London: Victor Gollancz, 1928).

dore Roosevelt and Wilson, put Adolf Hitler into power in Germany.

The British, in helping Hitler's armaments program, had intended that Germany would invade the Soviet Union, and that British and French forces would attack and occupy Germany from its rear, once German forces were bogged down in the Soviet Union. However, when London learned that Hitler was thinking of striking westward first, before attacking the Soviet Union, London dumped King Edward VIII and made concessions to the U.S.A., bringing the United States into the commitment to prepare for the coming war with Hitler.

Once Franklin Roosevelt was dead, London and its U.S. assets set the utopian strategy of Wells and Russell into motion, with the militarily unnecessary nuclear bombing of Hiroshima and Nagasaki. However, until President Truman could concoct the pretext for discharging General Douglas MacArthur, and as long as Dwight Eisenhower remained President, the growing utopian faction within U.S. military and related circles could not unleash the changes they intended to bring about.

The essential intent, as set forth by Wells, in the prefatory portion of a 1913 book, was the development and use of radioactive weapons as a force so terrible, that nations would surrender to world government, rather than be forced to fight a new major war. It was Russell who played the leading role in orchestrating the nuclear weapons-development programs of the 1940s, and it was Russell who defined the policy of "preventive nuclear warfare" which was put into motion with the 1945 bombings of Hiroshima and Nagasaki. It was the combination of air-power with sea-power, and the integrating of both with nuclear arsenals, which constituted the core of the military side of the Russell-led continuation of the Wells-Russell proposal for world government, as described by Wells in his 1928 **The Open Conspiracy**.

Following Eisenhower's retirement, the utopians gave us the "Bay of Pigs," the attempted 1962 assassination of France's President Charles de Gaulle, the Cuba missiles crisis of 1962, and the 1963 assassination of President Kennedy, which marked the typical footsteps toward putting U.S. policy under the apparently irreversible control of the utopian cause. The roles of John J. McCloy, Henry A. Kissinger, and Zbigniew Brzezinski, in dominating U.S. policy-directions during the interval from the Warren Commission Report until the retirement of President Jimmy Carter, merely typify the process which has led the U.S. to the present, self-inflicted global catastrophe of presently doomed world monetary-financial system.

Look at the minds of present two younger, post-World War II generations of adults. The connection among economy, education, and utopianism, is clearly demonstrated.

4. In Conclusion: Where the Empire Is Headed

With the 1989-1991 dissolution of Soviet power, the utopian-influenced circles of Prime Minister Margaret Thatcher and President François Mitterrand launched the demand that this development of 1989 be taken as the occasion for virtually destroying a Germany which, according to them, must not be reunified. The United States did not concur with all of the features of this Anglo-French savagery, but a compromise was reached, in which many of the intentions of Thatcher and Mitterrand were interwoven with policies intended to be ultimately disastrous for both Germany and the emerging nation-states of Eastern Europe, Russia most emphatically included.

At the same time, leading circles in the U.S. and under the British monarchy, saw in these developments the opportunity to proceed rapidly toward establishing a form of world government, run by the relevant English-speaking powers, which would be an eternal empire, modelled upon the Roman Empire, but worldwide. That is the current state of the world, especially since Sept. 11, 2001. However, there is something else to be considered. The first Roman Empire was formed during a time that Rome was at the height of its powers. The new Empire being attempted presently, finds the English-speaking powers—the U.S.A., Canada, the United Kingdom, Australia, and New Zealand—at virtually the bottom of their descent into the worst global monetary-financial crisis since the 1648 Treaty of Westphalia. The irony of it all, is that the conditions under which the consolidation of the new empire is being attempted, are conditions created chiefly by more than three decades of lunatic utopians' efforts to destroy the institutions upon which the former power of the U.S.A., western Europe, and Japan had depended up to and slightly beyond the mid-1960s.

Since the Baby Boomers came of college age, back during the mid-1960s, we now have two-plus generations, which, with a crucial minority of exceptions, were better described as two-plus successive degenerations. They were destroyed, culturally and otherwise, each generation to a greater degree than the next, looted of their natural human potential to assimilate both a Classical humanist development of their creative powers, and matching productive potentialities. The current younger adults and adolescents, are fairly described as either the "punk generation," or, simply, the "no-future generation."

This has been compounded by the correlated effects of transforming the leading economies of the United States and Germany, among others, from producer societies, into increasingly decadent consumer societies. This is a process accompanied by both willful destruction of vital productive capacities, and the looting, through attrition, of essential basic economic infrastructure.

This is what the Benthamites did to the English population, to produce the rot to which Babbage, Herschel, and Peacock referred. This is producing presently, a rot matched by the proliferation of armies of lunatics, more like the Flagellants of the Fourteenth-Century New Dark Age, than the pitiful, butchered wretches of Wellington's "Peterloo" and the Luddite lunacies.

Typical is the case of the hordes of victims of a socially-induced form of mass schizophrenia, the violence-prone video-games addicts typified by the slaughters at Columbine and Erfurt. These pre-trained "point-and-shoot" cannon-fodder are on the production-line to become the ground meat processed as the neo-Roman legionnaires of a global, perpetual "Clash of Civilizations" war. Because of the characteristics of a socially-induced mass-schizophrenia generated by such methods, they are as likely to butcher one another as their designated targets, a phenomenon which can not long be concealed under the dubious euphemism of "friendly fire."

The utopian policies underlying these patterns reflect, chiefly, two things to be emphasized as the conclusion of this report. First, they reflect the intention of utopians of the Wells-Russell genre, to create utopias in which populations are bred, trained, and culled, to serve as willing human cattle for their feudal-like masters. Drugs and video-game-induced mass-schizophrenia, complemented by what are termed euphemistically psychotropic drugs, will keep the human cattle dumb and manageable. Second, they reflect that the would-be masters of such utopias are intellectually, culturally in-

EIRNS/Christopher Lewis

The red-light district in Frankfurt, Germany, located conveniently next to the banking center. The economies of the United States and Germany, among others, have been transformed from producer societies, into increasingly decadent consumer societies.

capable of maintaining the empire over which they intend to reign.

When the Benthamites did what they did to the hapless population of the United Kingdom, powerful civilizations were rising from the rubble created by the Jacobin Terror, by Napoleon Bonaparte's fascist legions, and by the Congress of Vienna. England was forced to adapt to the reality of developments in the world at large. Today, by lurching toward consolidating a global imperial system, the utopian tyrants' nations doom themselves, by seeking to crush, one after another, each and all of those cultures from which the challenge might come to cause a regeneration within what are threatening to become the self-doomed cultures of the English-speaking world.

There is no possible way the utopians could win, but, unless they are stopped, the entire world will lose.

What happens, therefore, is up to you.

EDITORIAL

To Stop the War Party, Shut Down the British System

April 16—The majority of the world's nations and peoples are in a state of shock, and fear, that the recent 180 degree turn by President Donald Trump—from his rejection of "regime change" and a commitment to work with Russia and China for peace and development, to a criminal and unwarranted military attack on Syria and a threat to preemptively attack North Korea—could provoke a global nuclear war at virtually any moment. This fear is fully justified, but to prevent such an existential disaster for mankind, they must finally come to terms with the fact, long identified by Lyndon LaRouche, that the source of this crisis is the British Empire and the British System.

Not only did the *London Guardian* brag on April 13 that Britain's GCHQ (the UK's NSA equivalent) first notified the US intelligence services of so-called suspicious contacts between Trump campaign personnel and Russians deemed to be "suspected intelligence agents"—as if contact with Russians were a bad thing—but they openly complained that the United States was prohibited by law from spying on their own citizens—so the Brits had to do it for them.

Through their influence over political and media networks in the U.S., and their primary asset George Soros, the British used a totally fake dossier fabricated by "former" MI6 agent Christopher Steele to create a "color revolution" movement against the Trump Presidency over supposed ties to the Russians. Then, using fake intelligence reports from their terrorist-connected "White Helmet" assets in Syria, the British surrounded Trump with the lie that the Syrian government had used chemical weapons against their own population—an absurdity, since it served no military purpose, and the Syrian government was already clearly winning the war against ISIS and al-Qaeda terrorists with Russian help. Recall that it was Tony Blair who provided the fake intelligence that Saddam Hussein had weapons of mass destruction, drawing GW Bush into the war on Iraq that launched the current Hell, of terror, and a mass exodus of refugees across the Middle East.

This British complicity was made public on April 12 in the UN Security Council, when Russian Deputy Envoy to the Security Council, Vladimir Safronkov, turned directly to the British Ambassador, Matthew Rycroft, who had just denounced Russia for backing Bashar al Assad in Syria (and who had earlier been an aid to Tony Blair when the British launched the criminal war on Iraq). Safronkov correctly identified the British motive in their lies and war mongering: "You are afraid that we might work with the U.S. This is what you lose sleep over."

This is exactly the British purpose. The British have used the United States as their "dumb giant" to fight their colonial wars ever since the assassination of John F. Kennedy—from Vietnam to Iraq to Libya and Syria, and now perhaps North Korea, which would bring all of Asia and the world into a nuclear holocaust. The British are willing to risk global nuclear war in order to prevent the U.S. from rejecting the imperial division of the world into conflicting East and West, from uniting the entire world behind mutual peace and development, and ending Empire once and for all.

LaRouche's Schiller Institute demonstrated the

way out of this disaster on April 13-14 in Manhattan, in a conference titled "U.S.-China Cooperation on the Belt and Road Initiative and Corresponding Ideas in Chinese and Western Philosophy." Speaking at the conference were leading Chinese and Russian diplomats and professionals, presenting the urgency of President Trump joining with China and Russia in the New Silk Road projects now bringing win-win development, rather than war, to every part of the world. Helga Zepp-LaRouche, founder of the Schiller Institute, addressed both the urgency of this cooperation as the necessary "war avoidance" policy, but also the need to bring the cultural traditions of all great nations—and especially those of the Chinese Confucian culture and the Western Renaissance culture—into harmony as the basis for meeting the common aims of mankind.

This requires, at long last, the completion of the U.S. Revolution against the British imperial system, crushing that evil system within the United States and worldwide, now, before they succeed in launching a war that would mean the immediate end of civilization as we know it.

All citizens, of all nations, must act on the basis of their true humanity—at this moment of crisis of civilization—to join with the LaRouche movement and other like-minded citizens of the world, to crush the British system, and bring into being a new paradigm represented by the New Silk Road process of peace through development.